A RETREAT WITH JOHN THE EVANGELIST

# Other titles in the
# A Retreat With... *Series:*

# A Retreat With John the Evangelist

## That You May Have Life

Raymond E. Brown, S.S.

ST. ANTHONY MESSENGER PRESS

Cincinnati, Ohio

*Nihil Obstat:* Rev. Ralph J. Lawrence, O.F.M.

*Imprimi Potest:* Rev. John Bok, O.F.M.

*Imprimatur:* +Most Rev. Carl K. Moeddel, V.G.
    Archdiocese of Cincinnati
    April 27, 1998

The *nihil obstat* and *imprimatur* are a declaration that a book is considered to be free from doctrinal or moral error. It is not implied that those who have granted the *nihil obstat* and *imprimatur* agree with the contents, opinions or statements expressed.

Scripture translations are Raymond E. Brown's own translation, as found in his Anchor Bible (Doubleday) commentaries on John and the Johannine Epistles, with modifications.

Cover illustration by Steve Erspamer, S.M.
Cover and book design by Mary Alfieri
Electronic format and pagination by Sandy L. Digman

ISBN 0-86716-353-4

Published by St. Anthony Messenger Press
Printed in the U.S.A.

# DEDICATION

*To the interrelated families*
*SULLIVAN, DODDS, O'CONNOR and GRYCZ*
*with thanks for many personal kindnesses,*
*and above all for what they have taught me by*
*example about Christian love for one another*

# Contents

# Introducing A Retreat With...

Twenty years ago I made a weekend retreat at a Franciscan house on the coast of New Hampshire. The retreat director's opening talk was as lively as a long-range weather forecast. He told us how completely God loves each one of us—without benefit of lively anecdotes or fresh insights.

As the friar rambled on, my inner critic kept up a sotto voce commentary: "I've heard all this before." "Wish he'd say something new that I could chew on." "That poor man really doesn't have much to say." Ever hungry for manna yet untasted, I devalued any experience of hearing the same old thing.

After a good night's sleep, I awoke feeling as peaceful as a traveler who has at last arrived safely home. I walked across the room toward the closet. On the way I passed the sink with its small framed mirror on the wall above. Something caught my eye like an unexpected presence. I turned, saw the reflection in the mirror and said aloud, "No wonder he loves me!"

This involuntary affirmation stunned me. What or whom had I seen in the mirror? When I looked again, it was "just me," an ordinary person with a lower-than-average reservoir of self-esteem. But I knew that in the initial vision I had seen God-in-me breaking through like a sudden sunrise.

At that moment I knew what it meant to be made in the divine image. I understood right down to my size eleven feet what it meant to be loved exactly as I was. Only later did I connect this revelation with one granted to the Trappist monk-writer Thomas Merton. As he reports in *Conjectures of a Guilty Bystander*, while standing all unsuspecting on a street corner one day, he was overwhelmed by the "joy of being...a member of a race in which God Himself became incarnate.... There is no way of telling people that they are all walking around shining like the sun."

As an absentminded homemaker may leave a wedding ring on the kitchen windowsill, so I have often mislaid this precious conviction. But I have never forgotten that particular retreat. It persuaded me that the Spirit rushes in where it will. Not even a boring director or a judgmental retreatant can withstand the "violent wind" that "fills the entire house" where we dwell in expectation (see Acts 2:2).

So why deny ourselves any opportunity to come aside awhile and rest on holy ground? Why not withdraw from the daily web that keeps us muddled and wound? Wordsworth's complaint is ours as well: "The world is too much with us." There is no flu shot to protect us from infection by the skepticism of the media, the greed of commerce, the alienating influence of technology. We need retreats as the deer needs the running stream.

## An Invitation

This book and its companions in the *A Retreat With...* series from St. Anthony Messenger Press are designed to meet that need. They are an invitation to choose as director some of the most powerful, appealing and wise mentors our faith tradition has to offer.

Our directors come from many countries, historical

eras and schools of spirituality. At times they are teamed
to sing in close harmony (for example, Francis de Sales,
Jane de Chantal and Aelred of Rievaulx on spiritual
friendship). Others are paired to kindle an illuminating
fire from the friction of their differing views (such as
Augustine of Hippo and Mary Magdalene on human
sexuality). All have been chosen because, in their
humanness and their holiness, they can help us grow in
self-knowledge, discernment of God's will and maturity
in the Spirit.

Inviting us into relationship with these saints and
holy ones are inspiring authors from today's world,
women and men whose creative gifts open our windows
to the Spirit's flow. As a motto for the authors of our
series, we have borrowed the advice of Dom Frederick
Dunne to the young Thomas Merton. Upon joining the
Trappist monks, Merton wanted to sacrifice his writing
activities lest they interfere with his contemplative
vocation. Dom Frederick wisely advised, "Keep on
writing books that make people love the spiritual life."

That is our motto. Our purpose is to foster (or
strengthen) friendships between readers and retreat
directors—friendships that feed the soul with wisdom,
past and present. Like the scribe "trained for the kingdom
of heaven," each author brings forth from his or her
storeroom "what is new and what is old" (Matthew
13:52).

## The Format

The pattern for each *A Retreat With...* remains the
same; readers of one will be in familiar territory when
they move on to the next. Each book is organized as a
seven-session retreat that readers may adapt to their own

schedules or to the needs of a group.

Day One begins with an anecdotal introduction called "Getting to Know Our Directors." Readers are given a telling glimpse of the guides with whom they will be sharing the retreat experience. A second section, "Placing Our Directors in Context," will enable retreatants to see the guides in their own historical, geographical, cultural and spiritual settings.

Having made the human link between seeker and guide, the authors go on to "Introducing Our Retreat Theme." This section clarifies how the guide(s) are especially suited to explore the theme and how the retreatant's spirituality can be nourished by it.

After an original "Opening Prayer" to breathe life into the day's reflection, the author, speaking with and through the mentor(s), will begin to spin out the theme. While focusing on the guide(s)' own words and experience, the author may also draw on Scripture, tradition, literature, art, music, psychology or contemporary events to illuminate the path.

Each day's session is followed by reflection questions designed to challenge, affirm and guide the reader in integrating the theme into daily life. A "Closing Prayer" brings the session full circle and provides a spark of inspiration for the reader to harbor until the next session.

Days Two through Six begin with "Coming Together in the Spirit" and follow a format similar to Day One. Day Seven weaves the entire retreat together, encourages a continuation of the mentoring relationship and concludes with "Deepening Your Acquaintance," an envoi to live the theme by God's grace, the director(s)' guidance and the retreatant's discernment. A closing section of resources serves as a larder from which readers may draw enriching books, videos, cassettes and films.

We hope readers will experience at least one of those

memorable "No wonder God loves me!" moments. And we hope that they will have "talked back" to the mentors, as good friends are wont to do.

A case in point: There was once a famous preacher who always drew a capacity crowd to the cathedral. Whenever he spoke, an eccentric old woman sat in the front pew directly beneath the pulpit. She took every opportunity to mumble complaints and contradictions— just loud enough for the preacher to catch the drift that he was not as wonderful as he was reputed to be. Others seated down front glowered at the woman and tried to shush her. But she went right on needling the preacher to her heart's content.

When the old woman died, the congregation was astounded at the depth and sincerity of the preacher's grief. Asked why he was so bereft, he responded, "Now who will help me to grow?"

All of our mentors in *A Retreat With...* are worthy guides. Yet none would seek retreatants who simply said, "Where you lead, I will follow. You're the expert." In truth, our directors provide only half the retreat's content. Readers themselves will generate the other half.

As general editor for the retreat series, I pray that readers will, by their questions, comments, doubts and decision-making, fertilize the seeds our mentors have planted.

And may the Spirit of God rush in to give the growth.

*Gloria Hutchinson*
*Series Editor*
*Conversion of Saint Paul, 1995*

## An Introductory Word From the Editor

When we decided to include the four evangelists among our retreat directors, I could think of no more likely candidate to write *A Retreat With John the Evangelist* than Father Raymond E. Brown, S.S. He has spent the better part of the last forty years immersing himself in John's Gospel. It has soaked into his skin, permeated his skull and become second nature to this distinguished Scripture scholar.

However, commissioning a retreat by Brown based on John wasn't easy. In the manner of a certain Teacher from Nazareth, Brown turned my proposal upside down. What if he were to do a retreat by John facilitated by Brown as the "Translator"? Just suppose that the author were to soar off on the wings of imagination to rendezvous with a mysterious first-century figure who turned out to be the Evangelist? Then Brown could "interview" this enigmatic person and translate his Greek commentary into English.

That commentary—along with the Translator's observations—would become our retreat "conferences." I leave any further explanation in the capable hands of the Translator (Brown) and the Evangelist ("John"), though I am reminded that is not his name.

# Getting to Know Our Director

## An Introductory Word From the Translator

As the editor of the series told you, I encountered the Evangelist responsible for the Fourth Gospel. I shall not even try to explain how. I had spent more than half my life studying the Gospel according to John and the Epistles of John, but nothing prepared me for this experience. What an unusual character! When he heard that in my plan to write this retreat volume I was going to include a preliminary word about him, he insisted on including a preliminary word about himself. (Actually I am glad that he did; it enables you to judge for yourself how testy he can be.)

He does not read English and he does not totally trust what I am likely to say about him, even though I assured him it was harmless. His maternal language is Aramaic, but he speaks Greek with perfect confidence; and it is from that language that I have translated this retreat. (Frankly, his Greek, while correct, is a bit common; and his accent is noticeably Semitic.) I warned him that in his introductory "word" and elsewhere, he was speaking colloquially, and that he might offend readers who would have a very reverential attitude toward him. He told me off in no uncertain terms: Who was I, twenty centuries out of date (and there I was thinking that he might be out of date!) to tell him how to speak? After that I simply notified him from time to time when I was using a modern colloquialism to render his speech, and indeed he seemed to like our colorful equivalents.

He himself will report to you that I got off on the wrong foot in several ways, especially by asking about his identity, and by comparing his Gospel to others. He told me with an air of superiority that the group of which he was a member (those whom scholars call "Johannine Christians") did not use the term "Gospel" (translating the Greek *euangelion*, "good news"), but "Message" (translating the Greek *angelia*). I argued with him because I did not want to translate a whole retreat using "Message" or its equivalent, "News, Announcement." That would sound like Western Union, a newspaper or a wedding invitation. My sarcasm was wasted since those comparisons were not part of his world.

But I had to compromise in his favor: I would use a compound term "Gospel Message" in quotation marks for what we call the Gospel according to John and no other work would be thus designated. (As you will see, he did not forget the issue, because he refers from time to time with a bit of a jab to "those other works you call Gospels.") He thus won his struggle to have a New Testament category of his own—even if, as he will tell you, when we began our conversation, he had no idea of what our scriptural New Testament was.

To keep him happy I had to assure him that, while in the three other Gospels there were many wonderful things about Jesus, his "Gospel Message" was still treasured as the only one of the four to make clear the Word became flesh—indeed that he had contributed to our language the key theological term and concept of "incarnation." (The fact that we had developed a term from Latin rather than from Greek amused him. For him the Romans knew how to run things, but they did not have much culture.) It did not help that I had to warn him that some of those who would want to make the retreat with him might not have read his Gospel thoroughly. I told him I had written commentaries on his Gospel and I would suggest one or the other of these and other books to readers who did not know the Gospel. That idea was not appreciated: He was not enthusiastic about letting himself be used for promoting anybody else's writing.

All this was child's play compared to communicating to him the idea of a retreat. "Why would one want special thoughts about God and Jesus over seven days? Did not one think about them every day?" In such comments I was never quite sure when he was pulling my leg to put me in my place. But fortunately through concessions of eliminating what he regarded as nonsense, at last he consented to talk about Jesus in a way that could be fitted into a retreat format. Indeed, he seemed to become enthusiastic about explaining ideas from his "Gospel Message" to people of my time. Occasionally when I related to him questions we might have, he would direct his remarks to answer them. I could not get him, however, to make his conferences of equal length. At times he was brief when I wished he would be more expansive. Yet, and I hope God and you will forgive me, at other times, having struggled to get him to speak, I wished I could get him to stop—especially when he began to criticize other Christians of New Testament times.

In particular, I bowed to one of his absolute demands: Once he began to speak for the record (i.e., all the chapters to come in this book), I was to translate literally, not to soften a word. So far as he was concerned my ideas were likely to be "from below," whereas his perceptions were true to what was "from above." Thus you will hear from him as he is, "warts and all." My only contributions (he would add a question mark after "contributions") within his remarks are insertions in square brackets. These include chapter and verse references—the Evangelist was intrigued to find that his "Gospel Message" had been so mathematically dissected—introductory subsection headings, and a few explanatory phrases lest you miss his subtle (here, let me put in a question mark) references. I wanted to add a postscript chapter at the end of the retreat, but he vetoed that adamantly—he was going to have the last word.

Let me mention one other matter. Given historical simplifications that have probably shaped your own ideas, it may be wise for me to list explicitly the cast of people who produced the works identified by the name "John" in the New Testament—at least the cast as I can figure it out from the somewhat offhand references of my first-century dialogue partner:

- *"The Beloved Disciple"* or, more properly, "the Disciple whom Jesus loved." I asked several times for his name and was met with scornful silence by the Evangelist. He was a companion of Jesus but not one of the Twelve and seemingly no one named in any other New Testament book. Thank heaven that I bit back the question on the tip of my tongue, "Does that mean he was a minor disciple?" That would have resulted in an abrupt end of the conversation, because the Evangelist regarded him as the greatest of Jesus' disciples, the one who came to understand Jesus best. But this Disciple did not reach that exalted understanding during Jesus' lifetime; for I got the impression that his life as a follower of Jesus for decades after the resurrection brought an ever deepening understanding and love. I even caught a hint that in the better aspects of various characters described in the Gospel, male and female (the man born blind, Martha and Mary Magdalene), we were seeing aspects of the Beloved Disciple's own strengths. So far as the Evangelist was concerned, however, the Beloved Disciple's name was not necessary knowledge for us; Jesus the Good Shepherd knows all his own by name.

- *The Evangelist himself.* A disciple of the Beloved Disciple but one who had never himself seen or heard Jesus. For all that he knew about Jesus he was dependent on the Beloved Disciple (who was dead by the time the Gospel was completed) and on the Johannine community's reflections on the tradition that the Beloved Disciple had shaped. From one of his remarks I gather that the Evangelist knew also, at least in general, what other Christians were relating about Jesus—narratives similar to those in our Gospels according to Mark, Matthew and Luke, even though he had never read these three Gospels till I gave him a Greek New Testament. Clearly he judged his own "Gospel Message" to be superior to any other tradition about Jesus, but in fact he had rethought some of that other tradition and its traces remain. At the request of my Evangelist dialogue partner I have translated into Greek for him almost all that I wrote about him in this introductory "word" (except the barbs), but I will not translate what follows lest I add to the sense of superiority that he already feels. As we talked I realized even more clearly than I had from reading the Gospel what exquisite dramatic contributions he had made to the Jesus tradition. If the Beloved Disciple had plumbed the depths of the mystery of Jesus, the Evangelist had shaped it into an unforgettable "Gospel Message," to use his own term. In a very real way he understood that the message is the medium.

- *Someone who added to the Evangelist's "Gospel Message."* I knew my scholarly colleagues have been positing a redactor or editor of the Fourth Gospel who inserted into the Evangelist's composition a number of passages—whence some strange sequences in the narrative. Look, for instance, at 14:31 where Jesus urges that he and his disciples get up to leave the table of the Last Supper (hooking nicely into 18:1 where he and his disciples arrive at the garden across the Kidron), and yet he continues talking for three chapters, at times repeating what he has already said. The Evangelist seemed aware that there was some "tampering" with the "Gospel Message" after he had written it; and he seemed to have no trouble when, without identifying them, I mentioned words of Jesus in the Gospel that I knew scholars attributed to the redactor. Nevertheless, at an off-guard moment, he muttered something that can only be translated as a regret that people did not keep "their cotton-picking hands" off what was already done well. [Translator: I warned the Evangelist that the way his colorful Greek idiom was being translated equivalently into English could be deemed objectionable, but he insisted.]

- *Other Johannine writers,* indeed what we would call a school. The Evangelist was aware that there were what we call the Epistles of John even though they were written after he composed the "Gospel Message." He referred to the writers of those Epistles as his fellow disciples, occasionally agreed explicitly with sentiments found in them, and did not protest when in my own conversation I slipped in phrases from the Epistles. Indeed he regarded I John as a type of commentary on his own "Gospel Message." Yet it was clear that the problems those writers were facing were different from the problems reflected in his own work.

If listing all those people seems complicated, do not worry, dear readers. There are only two figures who will emerge with any prominence in the retreat that follows: the Evangelist himself as one of the most original Christian thinkers of all time, and the object of his total devotion, Jesus the Messiah, the Son of God, about whom he wrote that *you* may have life.

## An Introductory Word From the Evangelist

Giving this "retreat" is a strange experience for me. I had to depend for so much, including a knowledge of you who will read this, on what your Translator told me. (I don't fully trust his judgment, and I would much rather have seen your situation with my own eyes.) First I had to find out what a retreat was. Frankly, this "retreat" business seemed a lot of fuss about what should be obvious. We need to spend time with Jesus—we need to "remain" with him—if we are going to bear fruit and have life [15:4-7].

But when your Translator explained to me all the techniques you have developed for this (a special week, prayers, conferences, reflections), I wanted to bow out. "You have made it too complicated," I complained to the Translator. He even wanted to call me "the Director"—I have never directed anything in my life. I must have scared him because he then became more reasonable in his demands. I was to talk about Jesus, and he would compose only a few prayers drawing on the "Gospel Message" (which he insists on calling a Gospel) and add some contemporizing applications. Later on I asked him to read back to me in Greek—his accent is bizarre—a few of the prayers. They are OK; at least they are not mushy or too long. As for his applications, I could do better myself if only I knew your situation.

But I am getting ahead of myself. Before he ever started discussing this "retreat," the first thing your Translator said on encountering me was "Are you John the Evangelist?" That threw me; for my name does not happen to be John, and I was not sure precisely what this title "Evangelist" meant. Your Translator explained to me that since I forgot to put my name on what I wrote, many who had read it thought I was John, son of Zebedee. Actually that would have been nice: He was one of the most decent of the Twelve. But it doesn't happen to be so.

Then your Translator asked me, "Well at least are you the 'Beloved Disciple'?" That got my back up; I told him in no uncertain terms that I did not appreciate the "at least." Yet I was flattered to think that I should be identified with the greatest witness to Jesus, the Disciple whom he loved especially and who came to embody all that Jesus expected of his followers. But again it doesn't happen to be so: I am not the Beloved Disciple.

Then your Translator recounted to me all the other guesses about my identity, covering practically everyone mentioned in my "Gospel Message." Some even thought I was a woman. Actually I like women, and we had some wonderful women in our community; but I am not one of them. I could see I was annoying your Translator.

"Well, then," he said, "if you are not John, son of Zebedee, nor the Beloved Disciple, nor someone named in the Gospel Message, just who are you?" I told him he sounded like the emissaries of the Pharisees putting John the Baptist on the grill [1:19-22].

Finally I turned and put a question to him: Does it really make much difference what my name is? That query was more apropos than I realized, because later when he showed me that odd collection of early books you call the New Testament, I looked through all those books in vain for my real name. Believe it or not, I am not even mentioned by name in there! (That absence should warn you folks how limited in scope your collection is. Imagine, no one remembered me.) I realized then that if I had given the Translator my name, he would have insulted me by reporting he never heard of me. But the real point of my question was that you who follow the retreat should be interested in Jesus, not in me. Like my fellow disciples I am only a witness.

But to come back to my puzzlement about "John the Evangelist," what did this "Evangelist" mean? That was when I found out that you people were reading over and over again four works about Jesus that you called "Gospels" and that my writing was being treated as one of the four. My face must have betrayed my astonishment at such a failure to recognize the uniqueness of my work, for your Translator hurried to assure me that my writing was treated differently from the others in the readings that accompanied your eucharistic celebrations—in a pattern of three years the others got only a year apiece, whereas my writing was read every year and in the most sacred part of the year. I'll have to take his word that mine is considered the most spiritual and that I am known as the theologian par excellence. [Translator: I was thinking of the title "John the Divine," which means John the Theologian, but I was afraid he might take "divine" literally and rejoice at the thought.]

When the Translator found out that I had never seen the other three, he insisted that I read them in order to get some idea of what you would know. Frankly, that was a lot of bother; but I quickly recognized that they were forms of a basic story of Jesus that had been circulating in many churches in my lifetime. In point of fact I wrote my "Gospel Message" (which your Translator persists in calling a Gospel) to bring out a different view of Jesus that the widely circulated story was neglecting because it lacked the guidance of the Beloved Disciple. Reading those three "Gospels," which at first seemed a waste of time, was what led me to agree to give you this retreat, as you call it. If you are classifying my "Gospel Message" with those other works and are even slightly tempted to put it on the same level as you put them, you need some guidance. Even if I say so myself, my work is more perceptive about Jesus—just as the Beloved Disciple was more perceptive than all those others who according to your New Testament followed Jesus during his ministry.

I shall begin this retreat, therefore, by reflecting on the basic secret about Jesus that none of the writers of those "Gospels" seems to have understood. From that all my other reflections will flow.

# Day One

## The Secret of Jesus: The One Who Has Come

### Opening Prayer (Scripture for Reflection)

"The Word became flesh and made his dwelling among us." (John 1:14)

"God loved the world so much that He gave the only Son, that everyone who believes in him may not perish but may have eternal life." (3:16)

"I came that they may have life and have it to the full." (10:10)

## Retreat Session One

When I used to encounter other followers of Jesus—those other sheep who were not part of our [Johannine] fold but whom Jesus hoped would ultimately be one with us [10:16]—I often heard them talking about that future moment when the Son of Man would come from heaven to judge the world. I felt like crying out to them, "Don't you know he has already come from heaven for the judgment of the world?" So many of those others who loved Jesus and were proclaiming him seemed to start the story with his being baptized by John or even with his conception, as if there were nothing before that. They did not mention the glorious life he had with his heavenly Father before the world began [17:5]. But if people do not understand that, how can they understand the breathtaking extent to which God so loved the world? We say that God is love, but the way we know that love is through God's giving His only Son and sending him into the world [1 John 4:8-9]. Yes, God gave his only Son to become flesh and dwell with us [John 3:16; 1:14].

True, the Son will come back again from heaven, but more important for our understanding him (and God) is that he came from heaven in the first place. Because he was with God, he understood God; because he became flesh, he understands us. He is the bond of unity between God and human beings [17:21]. In telling Jesus' story other followers of Jesus have rightly emphasized how amazed people were at what he said and did, how he taught with authority and acted with extraordinary power. But I share with you the secret of that as Jesus himself explained it. All that he taught was what he heard when he was with God [7:16; 8:28; 12:49]. All that he did was patterned on what he saw when he was with God [5:19; 8:38].

We who were Jews prided ourselves that Moses could tell us God's will and commands because he had gone up Mount Sinai and spoken with God. But Jesus did not have to "go up" to be in God's presence because he was already there. He was God's word by which God spoke to Moses. Indeed, long before Moses he was the Word God spoke at creation. God said, "Let there be light"; and Jesus is the light of the world that God brought into existence through him [1:4-5,9; 8:12; 9:5; 12:46].

Moses was so proud that he could show people how to construct the Tabernacle or Tent that housed God's presence on earth because Moses had seen the design of that Tabernacle or Tent when he was in God's presence on the mountain. But when God's Word became flesh, he "tented" among us [1:14—the Greek for "dwelt" resembles the word for Tent/Tabernacle]. In other words, Jesus was the embodiment of God's presence among us.

God gave a great gift through Moses by establishing a covenant with the people of Israel: an act of spontaneous, unmotivated love that endured with fidelity as a sign of God's kindness despite all of Israel's failures. But how much more was the enduring love that came through Jesus Christ [1:17]. No one, not even Moses, had truly seen God as he was and is; but the only Son, who was himself God, revealed him. Indeed, whoever saw Jesus with the eyes of faith, saw his heavenly Father [14:9]. The realization that contact with Jesus meant contact with God was why we developed a slogan about the roots of our tradition: "We have heard, we have seen with our own eyes, we looked at and felt with our own hands the word of life" [1 John 1:1].

Perhaps now you begin to understand why I felt sorry for followers of Jesus who knew many wonderful things about him as the Messiah, the one described in the Law and the Prophets [1:41,45], but who had not penetrated the mystery of his origins. Nathanael whom Jesus praised as "a genuine Israelite" was one of the most perceptive of those people, even praising Jesus as the Son of God in the sense of being King of Israel [1:47,49]. Yet Jesus had to tell all these disciples that they had greater things to see [1:50], namely himself as the Son of Man who was the ladder of communication between heaven and earth [1:51].

Part of that communication stems from the fact of the

Son of Man being the Son of God. A child has life from a parent; God's Son had God's own life. "Just as the Father possesses life in Himself, so has He granted that the Son also possess life in himself" [5:26]. No matter how eminent a divine emissary he might be, were Jesus anything less than God's unique Son, he could not have brought God's life into the world. But he has brought that life as a gift to those who believe in him—an eternal life, so that everyone who receives it shall never die at all [11:26].

**[Jesus' way of speaking and Divine Wisdom].** The origins of Jesus are reflected in the way I remembered and described him in my "Gospel Message." Your Translator tells me that sometimes when my "Gospel Message" is rendered in your language, the words of Jesus are written in poetic format. That is perceptive. Of course, he did not speak in rhyme, but in our [Johannine] tradition he is remembered as speaking in a solemn, sacred style and in roughly rhythmic lines consisting of clauses of approximately the same length.

Why such a poetic or semipoetic style? In our Jewish Scriptures human beings communicate in prose, but God communicates in poetry because God's speech is more sacred than ours. In a number of scriptural books [Proverbs, Sirach, Wisdom] we hear the words of divine Wisdom, the Wisdom of God personified as a female [because both in Hebrew and Greek the word for *wisdom* is feminine]. Wisdom says, "The Lord created me at the beginning...before the earth was made" [Proverbs 8:22-23]; and, speaking of herself in the heavenly assembly of God, "From the mouth of the Most High I came forth" [Sirach 24:3]. Thus she is a form of God's Word who exists from the beginning [compare John 1:1], a pure effusion of the glory of the Almighty [Wisdom 7:25; John 1:14], the refulgence of eternal light [Wisdom 7:26; John 1:4,5,9]. Wisdom was present when God made the world as "the artificer of all," crafting things [Wisdom 9:9; 7:22; Proverbs 8:27-30; John 1:3]. In particular she brought life into the created world [Proverbs 8:35; Baruch 4:1; John 1:4].

While in one way Wisdom stayed with the Lord from whom she derives [Sirach 1:1; John 1:18], in another way she took pleasure to come down and be with the human beings in whose creation she had assisted, and in particular to set up her tent in Israel [Proverbs 8:31; Sirach 24:8; John 1:11,14]. Since she stemmed so uniquely from God, she spoke in poetry when she addressed people offering herself as divine revelation.

I have drawn out this comparison so that you could see that Jesus, the divine Word, is divine Wisdom come among us, the creatures he created. It is no surprise, then, that he speaks in a solemn, poetic, sacred style. Nor is it surprising that he speaks of himself frequently in the first person, "I am...." In those Gospels that your Translator gave me to read, I found Jesus speaking frequently about "The kingdom of God," meaning God's rule over our lives which Jesus had made present among us. Our tradition preferred to remember Jesus speaking as "I am...." [I am the way, the truth, the life, the light of the world, the bread of life, the good shepherd, the vine...] After all, he is the personal embodiment of God's rule— the place where God's rule was so perfect that he and the Father were and are one [10:30].

Comparably divine Wisdom often speaks in the first person [Sirach 24] as she walks among people teaching them divine truth [Proverbs 8:1-10]. Indeed, she invites them to her banquet, "Come and eat of my food and drink of the wine I have mixed" [Proverbs 9:5]; "Come to me all you who yearn for me and eat your fill of my fruits...the one who eats of me will hunger for more; the one who drinks of me will thirst for more" [Sirach 24:18,21].

This casts light on why Jesus is remembered as issuing virtually the same invitation: "You should be working for food that the Son of Man will give you...I myself am the bread of life. No one who comes to me shall ever be hungry, and no one who believes in me shall ever again be thirsty" [6:27,35]. This is no simple human way of speaking. When the police attendants who were sent to arrest Jesus came back empty-handed to the chief priests and Pharisees, their explanation was: "Never has a man spoken like this" [John 7:45-46]. Those words were truer than they could have realized. Jesus spoke as the divine Word, divine Wisdom, become flesh.

In our Jewish Scriptures one way divine Wisdom came among us was as the gift of the Law through Moses. People had to make a decision about accepting that Law. Moses, before he died, offered Israel a choice: "If you obey the commandments of the Lord your God that I enjoin on you today,...you will live; but if you turn away your hearts and do not listen...you will certainly perish" [Deuteronomy 30:16-18]. Picking up on that, in a famous ceremony of renewing the covenant at Shechem, Joshua challenged the people to serve the Lord according to the Law or to forsake the Lord [Joshua 24:14-28].

Similarly Jesus said of himself as the light come into the world, "Now the judgment is this:...All who practice wickedness hate the light and do not come near the light for fear their deeds will be exposed; but those who act in truth come into the light, so that it may be shown that their deeds are done in God" [John 3:19-21]. In other words, just as a decision about the Law represented a choice about being counted or not counted among God's own people, a choice about accepting Jesus now represents a decision about being God's own. "To his own he came; yet his own people did not accept him; but all those who did accept him he empowered to become God's children" [1:11-12]. Those who did accept Jesus became another "his own" for whom he showed his love to the very end [13:1].

But being confronted with the light of Jesus and having to make a choice is too passive a depiction. In the descriptions of divine Wisdom she does not wait to be accepted or rejected; she roams the streets seeking people, finding them and crying out to them [Proverbs 1:20-21; 8:1-4; Wisdom 6:16]. So also Jesus walked along, encountering those who would follow him, searching out people, and crying out his invitation in public places [John 1:36-39,43; 5:14; 7:28,37; 9:35]. Such activity on the part of Wisdom and on the part of Jesus produces a division: Some seek and find; some do not [Proverbs 1:28; 8:17; Sirach 6:27-28; Wisdom 6:12; John 7:34; 8:21; 13:33]. Much of the first part of my "Gospel Message" concerns the different encounters of Jesus and people.

I have spoken so much about personified divine Wisdom that you may be asking why Jesus is called "the Word" rather than "Wisdom." It is not simply because in Greek [and in Hebrew] *Word* is masculine and *Wisdom* is feminine. Rather the key is in the dynamic connotation of *word*. Theoretically one could possess wisdom without that affecting others. *Word*, however, involves not only the speaker but also an audience to be addressed. Thus when we [Johannine Christians] say in our hymn, "In the beginning was the Word...and the Word was God," we are describing a God who was bringing into being a creation that he would address, that he would be concerned about, that he would love, and that ultimately by incarnation he would become part of.

Once having entered the world, Jesus as the Word

incarnate *speaks* to people. That is why interaction or
encounter is an essential part of the life of Jesus. It is the
entry to receiving God's life, not only for those of my
time but for all people of all times. I shall give examples
of this in the following conferences.

## For Reflection:
## Translator's Contemporary Application

The Johannine Evangelist has emphasized the
importance of incarnation, namely, that the Word who
had existence and life with the Father before the world
began came down into our world and life. This has
become so much a part of Christian faith that probably
many readers will be startled that this idea is not found
with any clarity in the other Gospels. It is found
elsewhere in the New Testament, for example, in Paul's
letters and in the Epistle to the Hebrews; but John is the
only writing that has Jesus himself speak about his
previous life with God.

For most of the New Testament God's supreme act of
love is embodied in Jesus' self-giving on the cross.
Incarnation brings into the picture an earlier act of love:
the divine self-giving in becoming one of us. ("Earlier" is
from our point of view, since for God all aspects of the
giving of the Son constitute one divine action.) Indeed,
some theologians have so appreciated the intensity of
love in the incarnation that they have wondered whether
that alone might not have saved the world even if Jesus
was never crucified.

Yet if reflection on Jesus and encounter with him are
to help us with our lives, our consideration must include
more than his coming into the world. It must involve the
way he lived and the way he died; otherwise he would

not be sharing in and exemplifying a truly human life. John has references to the salvific character of Jesus' suffering and death, often in terms of Jesus' being lifted up on the cross: "So must the Son of Man be lifted up that everyone who believes in him may not perish but may have eternal life" (3:14-15; also 11:51-52; 1:29).

Nevertheless, it is to the other Gospels that we must turn to get a picture of Jesus' life of lowliness: how often he had no place to lay his head (Matthew 8:20), how as he journeyed he and his disciples were refused hospitality (Luke 9:52-53), how his own townspeople tried to kill him (Luke 4:28-29), how Herod wanted to kill him (Luke 13:31). John does not tell us the nitty-gritty of Jesus' ministry or indeed much about the suffering on the cross (mockery by crowds, chief priests and criminals; his crying out to God in agony).

One of the great gifts of having four Gospels in our New Testament canon is that they complement each other. (That is why, whether or not our Evangelist likes it, we have put the four Gospels on the same level of respect.) If John teaches us about the love of God exemplified in the incarnation, the other Gospels help us by spelling out what that love meant in the life lived by the Word-become-flesh, "in all things tested as we are, but without sin" (Hebrews 4:15).

## Closing Prayer

Almighty God, your Son told us, "Eternal life consists in this: to know you the one true God, and Jesus Christ, the one whom you sent." Teach us through your Son to appreciate that in fully seeing and hearing him, we are seeing and hearing you, so that whoever believes in your Son receives your own life.

# Day Two

## Encounter: Understanding and Misunderstanding Jesus

### Opening Prayer (Scripture for Reflection)

"My sheep hear my voice; and I know them and they follow me." (John 10:27)

"His mother gave the instruction, 'Do whatever he tells you.'" (2:5)

Jesus answered (to Nicodemus), "You hold the office of teacher in Israel, and still you don't understand these things?" (3:10)

## Retreat Session Two

I began my talks with you by stressing that Jesus had come from God because all that he means for you stems from that. I pointed out that he walked among us as divine Wisdom incarnate, God's Word become flesh; and that is illustrated in the solemn, poetic style of speech characteristic of Jesus in my "Gospel Message." However, I must explore this point further if you are to understand how people encountered and still encounter Jesus.

The one who was divine Son of God and Son of Man came from above and entered a world that was alien to him. Even though his presence was a sign that God loved the world [3:16], Jesus did not belong to this world [17:14,16]. Yet, since he was truly flesh, the divine Word had to speak in human language, our language, the language of this world. This was not easy because the realities about which he spoke were of another world. He had to phrase the realities of above in language from below [3:31].

How could he do that? Jesus used what people regard as important and gave such things new meaning: life, light, birth, food. All these things are valuable and necessary, but the heavenly counterparts are of much more value. Indeed it is the heavenly that is true and genuine. This was very difficult for people to understand, for they heard Jesus speaking in terms they thought they understood when actually he was referring to other realities. Scene after scene in my "Gospel Message" illustrated that.

I shall speak of those scenes now, and you will see before you a whole cast of characters: his disciples, his mother, Jews concerned with the Temple sanctuary, Nicodemus, "the Jews" who reacted to his healing a lame man on the Sabbath; and especially my favorite three: the Samaritan woman, the man born blind, and the family at Bethany consisting of Martha, Mary and Lazarus.

These various characters had different types of encounters with Jesus reflecting their respective personalities and backgrounds. Yet in another sense each is a representative of all women and men. Your Translator tells me of a figure in much later literature who was known as "Everyman," a character in a play who stood for everybody. The characters I describe are like that.

Therefore in some way the readers of my "Gospel Message" are to see themselves in each of these upon whom I shall reflect with you. Jesus' encounters with them may help you to understand him.

**[The first disciples].** At the beginning of my "Gospel Message," I described Jesus' encounter with disciples of John the Baptist who in turn would become Jesus' disciples. The Baptist's task had been to testify to Jesus in order to reveal him to Israel [1:7,31], and he fulfilled that task when he pointed out Jesus to two disciples who in turn spoke of him to other disciples [1:35,41,43,45]. Here let me call attention to how Jesus dealt with them when they started following him—I do not mean simply walking along with him but committing their lives to him.

His first question was "What are you looking for?" [1:38]. That is still the first question he asks of all who would be disciples. He is always looking for us, but do we understand what our true needs are? The first disciples answered, "Where are you staying?" and he said, "Come and see" [1:38-39]. We must be willing to *stay* with Jesus a while and *see* for ourselves who he is and what following him means.

The former disciples of John the Baptist (one of them, Andrew), after staying with Jesus one day, already recognized that he was the Messiah, the anointed king who would carry out God's plan [1:40-41]. They did not keep that to themselves; and as they shared it with others, even deeper insights about Jesus emerged [1:45,49]. That is a fundamental factor in the following of Jesus: No one is given the gift of faith for himself or herself alone; whatever we come to know must be shared with others. The Word speaks through our words; and in proclaiming Jesus to others, we ourselves grow in perception.

**[Jesus' mother].** After calling his disciples, Jesus
encountered his own mother at Cana [2:1-11]. He was
about to move into a public ministry that would carry
him away from home, and his relationship to his family
had to be clarified. Jesus' mother recognized his unique
power and asked that he put it at the service of her
friends at a wedding. She was thinking on the level of
family needs and demands in which up to this time Jesus
had lived, that is, the level of this earth, so that an act of
benevolence was expected of Jesus.

But Jesus had a higher role dictated by his heavenly
Father's will with which he was fully in harmony. He had
not come to supply ordinary wine to assuage thirst, but to
bring divine realities. He could illustrate that when his
mother, having accepted Jesus' priority in ranking his
own destined hour ahead of her desire, instructed the
waiters to do whatever Jesus told them. He then changed
the water destined for Jewish purifications to a wonderful
wine and thus manifested his glory. This was a sign of
replacement. I shall speak later of his replacing the
significance of Jewish practices and feasts.

But for now I am interested in Jesus' mother as
representative of many who believe in him but with only
a limited understanding of what he really brings to us,
looking for earthly help as if it were more real than the
graces he brings us from God. Jesus' mother, however, in
her representative role goes beyond that, for she also
accepted Jesus' will ("Do whatever he tells you") and
thus illustrated discipleship. Jesus confirmed that in the
other scene in which she is remembered in our tradition.
As Jesus hung on the cross when his hour had finally
come, he made his mother the mother of our Beloved
Disciple and thus made her a figure that we would
always honor as preeminent in discipleship. Your
Translator tells me that she was honored by subsequent

Christians in many ways, but I would claim that the presentation of her in my "Gospel Message" was at the root of that recognition.

**["The Jews" of the Jerusalem Temple].** Another reaction to Jesus is dramatized by "the Jews" who saw Jesus drive out money changers and sellers from the Temple area [2:13-22]. When they asked for an authorizing sign, he answered, "Destroy this [Temple] sanctuary, and in three days I will raise it up." They thought he was talking about the physical building; but eventually, after his resurrection, we came to realize that he was talking about the sanctuary of his body to be raised from the dead.

Your Translator has told me that many are offended by what I have written in my "Gospel Message" about "the Jews"; frankly I have been misunderstood in some of that; but let me leave it till later. For the moment I am interested in "the Jews" in this scene only as examples of religious people who are offended when they see Jesus challenging religious practices they have come to accept. In that respect they could stand for religious people of all time.

As we look back, we can understand Jesus' anger at what he regarded as commercial abuses in the Temple area—an anger echoing the attitude of the prophets. In the ideal last times there was to be no commerce: "On that day there shall no longer be any merchant in the house of the Lord of hosts" [Zechariah 14:21]. But the offended "Jews" might well have replied to Jesus by asking how could the sacrifices be carried on without the purchase of animals and how could Temple taxes be paid without the proper coins (which required money changers). The presence of those who made this possible in the Temple area could be explained as a matter of convenience.

I am sure that in the long time period that separates

me from you, my readers, similar circumstances have occurred. Yet Jesus' attitude would be just as condemnatory if he faced them—unreasonable in the eyes of those who advocated logical compromises. Here we touch on an essential aspect of Jesus: Since he comes from another world, in this world he will always be a stranger from above. His thoughts and outlooks will always be different, even from the thoughts of us who are his followers. By that very difference Jesus challenges us to look to another and higher standard of values—his Father's standard.

We also see in this encounter how Jesus uses human language to convey his own ideas. When he spoke of the sanctuary, not only "the Jews" but also his own disciples who were present thought he was referring to the most sacred part of the Temple building that housed God's presence. It took the resurrection to make us realize that, once the Word became flesh, there was a new focus of God's presence. Jesus was now the sanctuary.

[Nicodemus]. The coming of Nicodemus to Jesus [3:1-36] offers a unique moment of reflection. Here was an educated man, a teacher in Israel, a Jewish authority who was involved in Sanhedrin meetings. He was not hostile to Jesus but was one of those at Jerusalem who had come to believe in Jesus because of the miracles he saw [2:23]. Nicodemus saw the physical side of Jesus' signs but not the fullness of what they signified. He saw Jesus as a wonderful teacher who had come from God in the sense that he had God-given power to perform miracles/signs; but he had not understood that Jesus had come from God as the creator Word become flesh, as divine Wisdom incarnate.

In my "Gospel Message" I described Nicodemus's struggle to understand Jesus. He probably thought that coming to Jesus to pay his respects would be received appreciatively, only to be told that he had not seen or entered the kingdom of God. What an insult to one who was part of God's chosen people through birth from a Jewish mother! Jesus uses the language of birth but tells Nicodemus that natural parents here below can only beget or give birth to natural life: "Flesh begets flesh" [3:6]. To enter the kingdom or rule of God, one has to be begotten or born from above through water and Spirit.

When your Translator had me read those other works you call Gospels, I found this saying of Jesus, "Amen, I say to you, unless you will turn and become like children, you will never enter the kingdom of heaven" [Matthew 18:3]. The one who reported that saying seems to have interpreted it in terms of having the disposition of a child, for example, in acknowledging dependency and need of God rather than having an attitude of self-sufficiency.

But our tradition saw in this type of speech by Jesus a much more profound sense: One must become like a child all the way, dependent for life itself; one must be begotten by God or born from God and receive life itself from God. Of course, Nicodemus misunderstood because he missed Jesus' play on begotten/born from above and could not picture himself being born again from his mother's womb. Nicodemus' understanding of birth and life were on the earthly level, but Jesus was speaking of greater realities and what he would call true birth and true life— God's own life given by God.

Now I have a chance of explaining more fully Jesus' challenge to you, my retreatants. When Jesus rebuked Nicodemus, "You hold the office of teacher of Israel, and still you don't understand these things?" [3:10], you probably nodded your head because, since you have been baptized, you thought you understood Jesus. But read on in my "Gospel Message" as Jesus describes all that he

said to Nicodemus as earthly things and announces that
he has yet to speak about heavenly things. Then he
speaks of himself as "the one who came down from
heaven—the Son of Man who is in heaven" [3:13]. You
may be asking yourself, "How can what Jesus has already
said about begetting from above be called earthly things?
How can Jesus have come down from heaven and still be
in heaven?" If you are puzzled in that manner, my
"Gospel Message" has done its work. No one of us fully
understands Jesus until at the end we shall be like him
and see God as he is [1 John 3:2]. Thus none of us is far
from Nicodemus, even if our lack of understanding is on
different issues.

Nicodemus's subsequent career is worth mentioning.
Our tradition did not recall just how he reacted after his
nighttime conversation with Jesus. Certainly he remained
attracted to Jesus; for when some of his fellow Sanhedrin
authorities condemned Jesus, he protested that Jesus had
not been given a hearing [7:50-52]. They ridiculed
Nicodemus's argument, but gave no indication that they
knew he was a disciple of Jesus. So during Jesus' public
career Nicodemus remained a secret admirer, not having
the courage to confess Jesus publicly.

I have little patience with such spiritual cowards, but
I give Nicodemus credit that eventually he did show
courage. When Jesus had died on the cross and many of
his known disciples were hiding out for fear of "the Jews"
[20:19], Nicodemus showed up with a wheelbarrow
[Translator: My modernization.] full of spices to put on
the body of Jesus for burial. If he first came to Jesus at
night, he was now out in the light as a disciple. And if a
hundred pounds of spices seems a bit overmuch, it made
up for his previous hesitancy. Jesus had foreseen this,
since he promised, "When I am lifted up from the earth, I
shall draw all to myself" [12:32]. And so Nicodemus can

offer hope to those of you who are hesitant about coming to Jesus and receiving—it is not too late.

**[The lame man].** While we are talking about different encounters with Jesus on the part of those whom I have called "Jews," let me turn to the very difficult encounter with those who criticized Jesus for healing the lame man at the pool of Bethesda on a Sabbath [5:1-47]. That fellow was not overly bright; after being healed, although he never found out Jesus' name, he went off and informed hostile fellow Jews of what Jesus had done.

Jesus did not apologize for "breaking" the Sabbath. Rather he pointed out that God works on the Sabbath [5:17]. People are born and die on the Sabbath, and only God can give life and take it away. Now the Father had turned over all such power over life and death to the Son, and so the Son could heal [give life] on the Sabbath. "The Jews" caught the implication but interpreted it as arrogant; they sought to kill Jesus because he was making himself God's equal [5:18]. Their misunderstanding is important because it made Jesus explain. He "made" himself nothing, for he could do nothing by himself—it is simply that the Father had given him everything. We call Jesus "Lord and God," and we recognize that he and the Father are one [20:28; 10:30]. Yet he would never claim anything for himself; a Jesus who was acquisitive or self-aggrandizing could not really represent a self-giving God. Rather Jesus was conscious that everything he had came from the Father, and so he could say, "The Father is greater than I" [14:28].

Much of Jesus' ministry was concerned with getting people to understand him as one who had come from God. But he never meant the knowledge to stop there. Understanding him would lead to understanding his Father. When Philip asked Jesus, "Show us the Father,"

Jesus answered, "Whoever has seen me has seen the Father" [14:8-10]. The eternal life that he brought consisted in knowing the one true God and the one whom he had sent—notice the order [17:3].

I have used these encounters to explain Jesus to you and to help you in your own struggles to understand him. There are more encounters that could help you to understand your own role as disciple. But that is enough for today; I'll talk about those other encounters tomorrow. Besides I can see that your Translator is itching to "clarify" my ideas, probably with his own examples of encounters since he has babbled to me about them. Well, unlike the bridegroom in my Cana story, I have served the choice wine first.

## For Reflection:
## Translator's Contemporary Application

I am tempted not to offer examples lest I give the Evangelist the satisfaction of having guessed correctly. Moreover, the implication that I shall serve up inferior wine was unnecessary. He may be right, but he did not need to rub it in. (There are moments when I regret getting involved in this retreat.) Oh well, here are two examples pertinent to encounter, as he predicted.

*First,* at the end of Day One, the Evangelist told us how the very nature of "the Word" involves an activity of speaking and the presence of an audience. That is important in the way we think about God. A story is told about a monk from one of the great Eastern non-Christian religious traditions who was curious about Christianity. He went to a missionary for information; but lacking time, the missionary brushed the monk off by handing him a copy of the Gospel according to John, telling him to read it and then come back.

A couple of months later the missionary happened to see this same monk on the street. Remembering him, the missionary asked whether the monk had read the Gospel. The monk said he had not because the first line, "In the beginning was the Word," puzzled and stalled him. "Why don't Christians think that in the beginning there was silence?" the monk asked. "You must have a noisy God!"

Well, in a way we do have a noisy God, a God who is outwardly oriented. On the opening page of the Bible, the very first thing we are told about God is that He spoke and things were created. Even John's Gospel, which is so reflective, does not concentrate on God's internal life but on God's relation to us. Only some years later and outside the New Testament, in the writings of Ignatius of Antioch (*Ephesians* 19:1), do we hear about God's silence.

*Second*, the Evangelist does not use the language of thinking about Jesus or meditating on him (which would be more familiar to us) but the need of encountering him. How can *we* do that? Jesus lived on earth some two thousand years ago, in another social situation and another place. Since the Evangelist feels free to guess what I am going to say, let me guess how he would respond (not too patiently) to that question. He would say, "That is why I wrote my 'Gospel Message.'" He wrote decades after Jesus lived; yet he did not write a series of meditations *about* what Jesus did and said. Rather in and through the Evangelist's pages Jesus himself acts and speaks. In our time through John's Gospel we have the same opportunity to encounter Jesus as did the Evangelist's first hearers/readers, for that work was written precisely to make Jesus present to people of all times [20:31].

Moreover, although I hate to flatter him, the Evangelist had the extraordinary dramatic ability to involve hearers/readers with Jesus, to draw them into the scenes described in the Gospel. A modern parallel I have found to exemplify the Evangelist's technique would probably displease him (if there was a way I could explain it to him) since it does not stem from highbrow literature.

My comparison is to Sir Arthur Conan Doyle's tales of Sherlock Holmes. His work constitutes an unusual case where the fictional character became more prominent in the readers' minds than the author. (There are Sherlock Holmes societies and fan clubs, not Conan Doyle clubs.) Part of the reason for that success was that the readers became involved in the plots trying to guess the solution, and in that process Dr. Watson played a role. The doctor, too, tried to find a solution but always unsuccessfully and thus became a foil for the readers. They recognized that Watson was wrong, and so they began to think that they understood the solution, only to be surprised by Holmes when he solved the case.

Similarly, in the encounters with Jesus described in John, readers see John's characters misunderstanding Jesus; and they begin to say to themselves, "That is not what Jesus means." When they do that and begin to offer their own solution, they have been trapped into participating in the dialogue with Jesus. Soon they find themselves surprised by him when he continues to speak from above. Then they have encountered Jesus.

## Closing Prayer

Almighty God, we are all different, mirroring the wonders of your creation. We approach you with different attitudes, some eager, some reluctant, some understanding, some misunderstanding. In your mercy you have given us Jesus so that we might encounter you in one like us.

Deal with us according to our differences, our strengths and our weaknesses, so that we may come to know you in him.

# DAY THREE

## Encounter: On Being a Disciple

### Opening Prayer (Scripture for Reflection)

"The water I shall give them will become within them a fountain of water leaping up unto eternal life." (John 4:14)

"I am the light of the world. No follower of mine shall ever walk in darkness; rather, that person will possess the light of life." (8:12)

"This sickness is not to end in death; rather it is for God's glory, that the Son of God may be glorified through it." (11:4)

## RETREAT SESSION THREE

I now want to talk to you about three extraordinary encounters with Jesus, involving the Samaritan woman at the well, the man born blind, and the family of Martha, Mary and Lazarus. I put a lot of time into crafting my "Gospel Message" account of them because, more than any other stories, they contain the key to discipleship.

**[The Samaritan Woman].** The first story, that of the Samaritan woman [John 4:1-42], illustrates the various obstacles that stand in the way of coming to Jesus in faith. The woman was smarting from the Jewish dislike for Samaritans, especially for Samaritan women who were regarded as impure. And that was her first obstacle to dealing with Jesus. "How can you, a Jew," she responded sarcastically, "ask me, a Samaritan woman, for a drink?"

This attitude made her a more realistic model for discipleship than if she were eager to encounter Jesus. After all, many people have a chip on their shoulder in regard to God because they see inequalities in life. Notice that Jesus did not answer her objection; he was not going to change instantly a whole world of injustice. Yet Jesus could offer something that would enable the woman to put injustice in perspective, namely, living water.

This is a good instance of what I explained previously: using the language of this world to talk about heavenly realities, and thus producing misunderstanding. Jesus meant water that gives life (a water symbolic of revelation, baptism); but misunderstanding him, the woman thought of flowing, bubbling water, contemptuously asking him if he thought he was greater than Jacob who provided a well [4:12]. (Is not "No thanks—I already have all I need" the first reaction of many people when someone tries to interest them in something new religiously?)

Ironically (and I expected most readers to recognize this), Jesus was greater than Jacob; but again Jesus refused to be sidetracked from his main goal. Ignoring the issue of who was greater, he explained that he was speaking of the water that springs up to eternal life, a water that will permanently end thirst. On a level of the convenience of not having to come to the well every day, that attracted the Samaritan woman. I suspect people will always be attracted to a religion that makes life more comfortable.

To move the woman to a higher level, Jesus shifted the focus to her husband [4:16]. She replied with a half-truth, only to have Jesus show that he was aware of her five husbands and of her live-in companion who was not her husband. Again that was a realistic touch, appropriate for reaching out toward all those whose obstacle to conversion is a far-from-perfect past. To be brought to faith people must acknowledge where they stand, but they can take hope from this story inasmuch as Jesus persisted even though he knew the woman's state. He did not say to the woman, "Come back after you straighten out your life," for the grace that he offered was meant to help her change.

Confronted with Jesus' surprising knowledge of her situation, the woman sought to escape by taking advantage of the fact that he was obviously a religious figure. Her question about whether to worship in the Jerusalem Temple or on Mount Gerizim [4:20] was a typical ploy designed to distract. When people encounter someone who probes their lives, they are often adept at bringing up as a distraction some old religious chestnut, so as to avoid making a decision. When was the last time this woman worried about such theological differences or even went up the mountain to worship?

Once more Jesus refused to be sidetracked. Although as a Jew he would maintain that Jews had an interpretation of God's salvific plan truer than that of the Samaritans, a time was coming, indeed was already here when such an issue was becoming irrelevant: Cult at both sites was being replaced by worship in Spirit and truth. Nimbly the woman tried one more ploy by shifting any decision to the distant future when the Messiah would come [4:25], but Jesus would not let her escape. His "I am he" confronted her with a current demand for faith.

If the Samaritan woman was slow in coming to understand Jesus, I would urge you with whom I am sharing these reflections not to feel superior. If you identify yourself as Jesus' disciple, consider that when Jesus' disciples returned [4:27], even though they had been with him for a while, they were no more understanding than the woman who met him for the first time. In my "Gospel Message" I used two stages to unfold the drama that followed. *Front and center* I pictured the disciples speaking with Jesus and misunderstanding his reference to food even as the woman had misunderstood the water imagery. When he spoke of the food that he already had to eat, they wondered if someone had brought him a sandwich! [Translator: My modernization.] Jesus had to explain: "My food is to do the will of the One who sent me" [4:34].

*On a side stage*, in the nearby village, I showed the woman, who was still not fully convinced, posing to the villagers the question, "Could this be the Messiah?" [4:29]. The villagers came and encountered Jesus for themselves so that their faith was not simply dependent on her narrative but on personal contact [4:42]. Quite frankly I wanted readers to surmise that by being instrumental in bringing others to believe, the woman's own faith came to completion—a not unusual occurrence. And at last she drank of the water of life.

**[The man born blind].** The second story, the healing of the man born blind [9:1-41], illustrates how faith grows amid trials. If the story of the Samaritan woman illustrated an initial coming to faith, this narrative shows that often first enlightenment does not result in adequate faith. In a previous retreat session I mentioned how the main character might also serve as a representative of all, indeed as an "Everyman." That is certainly true here. The initial dialogue where Jesus proclaimed, "I am the light of the world," served notice that more than physical sight is involved.

The basic story of the healing was simple. Jesus approached the blind man, anointed his eyes with mud mixed with saliva, and told him to wash in the Pool of Siloam. The man did so and came back seeing. I sprinkled the story with hints that would remind my hearers or readers of their own conversion and baptism. The blind man came to see the light by being "anointed"—well, anointing became a part of our baptismal practice very early, and "enlightenment" was a term for baptismal conversion. My readers could not miss the symbolism of water that restored sight, for I told them that "Siloam," the name of the pool, meant "the one sent," a frequent description in our tradition for Jesus.

Besides having those who hear or read my "Gospel Message" recognize elements of their baptism, their own enlightenment, more importantly I wanted them (and I want you) to be taught that a series of testings may be necessary before sight really comes. Only gradually and through suffering did the man born blind come to full faith and enlightenment.

There were at least four steps in his progress, each involving an encounter: (1) At first, when queried by the onlookers, the man born blind knew only that "the man they call Jesus" healed him [9:11]. (2) Then, brought before the Pharisees and pressed with theological questions, he advanced to the conclusion that Jesus was "a prophet" [9:17]. (3) Next, after being threatened with expulsion from the synagogue, he recognized that Jesus was a man "from God" [9:33]. (4) Finally, having been expelled, he encountered Jesus himself, who sought him out and now asked point-blank, "Do you believe in the

Son of Man?" It was then at last that the man said, "I do believe"—the baptismal confession required in our [Johannine] community [9:35-38].

Your Translator has told me how many centuries have passed since I wrote my "Gospel Message." In that period of time how many of those who had a traditional faith stemming from baptism came to believe in their hearts only when difficult decisions tested their faith in God and Christ? It was only then that they understood what it meant to say, "I do believe."

In addition, let me talk about the reaction of those who queried the man born blind, since we also learn about faith from them. His being healed produced a division [Greek *krisis*, whence English *crisis*] among those who interrogated him. That is not surprising, for in our [Johannine] view an encounter with Jesus or his work forced people to decide and align themselves on one side or the other. But the division caused among the Pharisees [9:13-17] because Jesus healed the blind man on the Sabbath is particularly interesting. I admired those Pharisees who decided that Jesus could not be sinful because he did such signs (healings), but I would like now to seek to understand the other Pharisees who decided that Jesus was not from God because he did not keep the Sabbath. I did not do that in my "Gospel Message," but I have given a lot of thought to it since. (Perhaps this may help with those of you offended by things I said about "the Jews.")

The thinking of the hostile Pharisees probably went along these lines: God commanded that the Sabbath be kept holy; our ancestors decided that kneading clay was menial work that violated the Sabbath; Jesus kneaded clay on the Sabbath, and so he violated God's commandment. (I would guess that over the years many faithful disciples of Jesus judged along similar lines if someone violated what they had been taught as a traditional interpretation of God's will.) They were offended when their decision was greeted with sarcasm by the man born blind.

The difficulty with such reasoning is the failure to recognize that all such interpretations of God's will, no matter how well intentioned, are phrased in our earthly language and thus conditioned. Those positions we regard as definitive tradition are *true, but in regard to the issues that were in mind when they were formulated.* The Hebrews as slaves in Egypt had to work with clay to make bricks for the Pharaoh, and so kneading clay would justly be classified as servile work forbidden on the Sabbath. But the people who made that classification scarcely thought of kneading a scrap of clay to open a blind man's eyes.

Jesus, coming from above, raised new religious issues and inevitably caused offense to those who attempted to solve those issues quickly on the basis of previous situations. I recognize now that it was not necessarily out of malice that many of the genuinely religious people of Jesus' time rejected him. He was Jewish and they were Jewish; but if Jesus came back in your time, he would then be equally offensive to many good religious people who identify themselves as his followers [Christians]. As one who has come from God, he challenges our earthly perceptions of God at any time and cautions us about applying religious judgments from the past, without nuance, to *new* situations.

Our story offers still other participants who can be instructive about discipleship: the parents of the man born blind [9:18-23]. The man born blind, who step by step was brought to sight physically and spiritually, was sharply contrasted with the opposing religious authorities, who could see physically but gradually became blind spiritually [9:40-41]. Yet of interest also were those who refused to commit themselves one way or the other and make a decision. The parents knew the truth about their son's being healed, but they refused to say anything about what Jesus had done for him lest they be thrown out of the synagogue.

Again, having been forced by your Translator to think of your situation, I think there must be in your time, in addition to those who decide for Jesus at a great cost to themselves and those who for various reasons do not believe in him, perhaps an even larger group of those who have been baptized and nominally accept Jesus but are not willing to confess him if it costs anything. To be honest, in my time I judged that failure as grave as to deny him. Perhaps those who act that way do not realize this, but they are serious failures in terms of proclaiming Jesus to the world and being witnesses to him as we are all charged to do [15:27].

[Lazarus]. The third story that I have chosen to illustrate discipleship, the raising of Lazarus [11:1-44], is the most difficult to explain. In my first story, the Samaritan woman remained close to Jesus at the well for much of the drama and entered into a fairly long dialogue with him. In the story of the man born blind, he said nothing to Jesus at the beginning, was not in contact with him through most of the scene, and exchanged words with Jesus only at the end in a moment of piercing light when he confessed Jesus. In the present story, Lazarus never says a word to Jesus (or anyone else) and appears only at the end. In each story we are dealing with a different stage of faith. The Samaritan woman illustrated an initial coming to faith; the man born blind illustrated an incipient faith that acquired depth only after testing; the Lazarus story illustrates *the deepening of faith that comes through an experience of death.*

To understand this, we have to follow the deepening comprehension personified in the story by the reactions to Lazarus's death on the part of the disciples, and of Martha and Mary. Like his sisters Martha and Mary, Lazarus was loved by Jesus; and so when he died, the disciples were troubled by Jesus' seeming indifference. They misunderstood when he spoke of Lazarus's sleep. As with blindness in John 9 (of which we are reminded in 11:37), life and death were being used to teach about earthly and heavenly realities.

Martha, who was the chief dialogue partner in the drama, already believed that Jesus was the Messiah, the Son of God, and that her brother Lazarus would participate in the resurrection on the last day. Yet hers was an inadequate faith. First, like Jesus' mother at Cana, implicitly she put a demand on Jesus at the human level of friendship, "If you had been here, my brother would never have died" [11:21]. (Some of "the Jews" had the same attitude: "Couldn't he have done something to keep this man from dying?" [11:37].)

Second, Martha hesitated when Jesus ordered Lazarus's tomb opened. Jesus could and did bring Lazarus back to earthly life, but that was not his purpose in having come to this world from above. A man brought back from the grave is not necessarily better off or closer to God than those who have not yet died. Jesus came to give life that cannot be touched by death, so that those who believe in him would never die [11:26]. True faith has to include a belief in Jesus as the source of unending life. Such immortality, however, could not come in Jesus' public ministry; it had to await Jesus' own resurrection.

The story of Lazarus's death had within itself signs of the deeper life still to come. Consequently there was more difficult symbolism in the Lazarus narrative than was present in the stories of the Samaritan woman and the man born blind—symbolism that I who narrated it do not pretend always to fathom. (The one from above at times remains a stranger to me as well.) I do not know, for instance, whether Martha and Mary came to understand fully Jesus' words, "I am the life" [11:25]. In another instance, the tradition I received reports that Jesus shuddered, seemingly with anger, when he saw Mary and her Jewish friends weeping [11:33,38]. Why did Jesus react in this way at what seems like well-intentioned grief? Was he disappointed that even faithful disciples could not grasp that the life he brought reduced the importance of death?

Your Translator asked me why Lazarus emerged from the tomb tied hand and foot with burial bands and his face wrapped in a cloth [11:44]. But that symbolism becomes clear when we remember the account of Jesus' tomb. Jesus rose to eternal life, never to die again; therefore he left behind in the tomb his burial wrappings and the piece that covered his head for which he had no further need [20:6-7]. Lazarus was brought back to life enveloped in burial clothes because he was going to die again.

Thus, although the raising of Lazarus was a tremendous miracle bringing to culmination Jesus' ministry, it was still a sign. The life to which Lazarus was raised is natural life; Jesus meant it to symbolize eternal life, the kind of life that only God possesses and that Jesus as God's Son made and makes possible.

I think this has meaning when people confront death as their own final test. Even after the struggles of initial faith (the Samaritan woman) and a faith made mature through testing (the man born blind), facing death often constitutes a unique challenge to the belief necessary to being a disciple. The finality of death and the uncertainties it creates cause trembling also among those who have spent their lives professing Christ. Indeed, among our small community of [Johannine] disciples, it was not unusual for people to confess that doubts had come into their minds as they encountered death.

As I read your New Testament which the Translator gave me, I found a remarkable passage written by Paul where he cries out that death is the last enemy to be overcome [1 Corinthians 15:26]. That was what I meant to symbolize when I placed the Lazarus story at the end of Jesus' public ministry. When confronted with the visible reality of the grave, all need to hear and embrace the bold message that Jesus proclaimed: "I am the life." Despite all human appearances, "Everyone who believes in me shall never die at all."

Jesus did not speak to the Samaritan woman of earthly water that we drink only to get thirsty again, but of the water that springs up to eternal life. In reference to the man born blind Jesus was not referring to a physical sight that people can possess without being able to perceive anything they cannot touch, but to an insight into heavenly realities. In the instance of Lazarus Jesus was not simply renewing a life that ends in the grave, but offering eternal life.

## For Reflection:
## Translator's Contemporary Application

The Evangelist clearly regards these three stories as his narrative masterpieces and as the most profound commentary he could offer on discipleship. Church tradition has confirmed the correctness of his judgment since for some sixteen hundred years in varying ways it has given them a special place in the Lenten preparation of people to be baptized, to become Jesus' disciples. For instance, already about A.D. 400, an observant nun named Etheria who went to Jerusalem as a pilgrim tells us that in Lent there the Saturday before Holy Week was set aside for the reading of the Lazarus story. Currently the three stories are read on the last Sundays of Lent in the first year of the liturgical cycle (with an encouragement to read them in the other two years of the cycle as well).

Many people, when challenged to encounter Jesus, have problems similar to those faced by the Samaritan woman. We can hear a voice saying, "Why should I bother about God? He has done me no favors. I was born poor, or I was born deformed and sickly, or I was born into a minority race or a people despised by others and without advantages. If God is good, why is this so?"

We who believe cannot tell them honestly that if they come to Jesus, all that will change (even as John avoided having Jesus say that). Yet we can tell them that Jesus has a gift of life that can impart meaning to our earthly lives no matter how disadvantaged—or advantaged. Yes, there is a message for the advantaged as well, for they are prone to feel no need for Jesus and may ask what can he do for them that is better than what they have received from their ancestors (or their own endeavors) by way of wealth, comfort, position or privilege.

Some will come to Jesus on the grounds that it can do no harm and might make them feel better; others will come to him aware that, despite material appearances, their lives are a mess, perhaps too much of a mess to have hope. Jesus' dealings with the Samaritan woman teaches us that he offers life to all those people; he cannot be turned aside from his purpose.

In many ways the scene in Samaria reminds me of Francis Thompson's magnificent poem "The Hound of Heaven." In different ways we seek to avoid Jesus:

"I fled Him, down the nights and down the days;
I fled Him, down the arches of the years;
I fled Him, down the labyrinthine ways
   of my own mind...."

Yet he follows:

"[T]hose strong Feet that followed, followed after.
But with unhurrying chase,
And unperturbèd pace,
Deliberate speed, majestic instancy."

Nevertheless, the church does not read John in Lent only
to encourage those who are going to be baptized. It insists
that this is also a time of renewal of baptismal
commitment. Most who call themselves Christians were
baptized as infants; their godparents professed faith for
them. But there is no way that we can escape making a
believing commitment of our own, especially once we
begin to realize what being a firm Christian costs, and
how much easier it is not to take church and religion too
seriously.

Even then, a commitment made sincerely at one time
of life may be threatened when we run up against an
unexpected obstacle. "If there is a God, how can he do
this to me when I have tried to serve him?" The story of
the man born blind is read in church *for us*. There is
variety among those who judge that man: Some are
tempted to believe in Jesus because of the healing; some
are firmly convinced that Jesus' behavior is not
reconcilable with their notion of God's law and how God
acts; the parents half believe but do not want to pay the
price; the man born blind finally comes to faith, not in the
first encounter but as a result of trials and rejections. A
similar variety of attitudes exists among us who are asked
to renew our baptismal faith and commitment.

Beyond that, no matter how often we renew our faith,

there is the supreme testing by death. Whether the death of a loved one or one's own death, it is the moment where one realizes that all depends on God. We have been cautious during our life to shield ourselves with bank accounts, credit cards and investments, and to protect our future with health plans, life insurance, social security and retirement plans. Yet there comes a moment when neither cash nor "plastic" works. No human support goes with one to the grave; and human companionship stops at the tomb. One enters alone.

If there is no God, there is nothing; if Christ has not conquered death, there is no future. The Lazarus story speaks to such a moment. The "tos" and "fros" of the reactions show struggle even among the disciples and those who love Jesus as they face death. The Lenten/Easter mystery of crucifixion and resurrection victory is the appropriate moment to reflect on the promise:

> "I am the resurrection and the life.
> Those who believe in me,
> even if they die, will come to life.
> And everyone who is alive and believes in me
> shall never die at all" (11:25-26).

## Closing Prayer

Almighty God, help us to be disciples of your Son. If we are struggling with faith and doubting whether we should believe, overcome our obstacles. If we believe, strengthen our faith when it is tested by the difficulties of life. And as we face the specter of death, grant us the grace to see that already we possess your life that death cannot touch.

# DAY FOUR

## Apostles; Church Foundation; Sacramental Institution

### Opening Prayer (Scripture for Reflection)

"I am the vine and you are the branches; those who remain in me and I in them are the ones who bear much fruit, for apart from me you can do nothing." (John 15:5)

"I solemnly assure you, no one can enter the kingdom of God without being begotten of water and Spirit." (3:5)

"Let me firmly assure you, if you do not eat the flesh of the Son of Man and drink his blood, you have no life in you. The person who feeds on my flesh and drinks my blood has eternal life." (6:53-54)

## RETREAT SESSION FOUR

After I finished the last session your Translator asked me a number of questions, and they have fed into this retreat session. I don't like his imposing his interests on me, but occasionally he does bring up important points.

**["Disciples," not "apostles"].** First, he asked me why I so stressed "disciples" and never mentioned "apostles." Well, only some people were apostles, and they had authority. When I read your New Testament, I found Paul very conscious of being an apostle, and listing apostles first among those privileged by God's gifts [1 Corinthians 12:28]. Indeed, when the apostles died, I understand that great attention was paid to the question of who would succeed to their authority. I can see why such a transfer would be important to communities familiar with the shepherding of an apostle. But our tradition was different in several ways. We stressed Jesus alone as the Good Shepherd, an estimation that created a distrust about all others who would be human shepherds [10:2,7-8,11].

More important for my purposes here, we were primarily concerned with Jesus' gift of the life of God, eternal life, not with any charisms that involved different roles in the community. Again when I read your New Testament, I found that besides listing apostles first, Paul listed prophets, teachers, miracle-workers, healers, helpers, administrators and speakers in tongues; and evidently they were fighting one another, for he had to compare the community to a body that needed different parts [1 Corinthians 12:4-31].

How much simpler our vine symbolism [15:1-6] that ignores different roles: Jesus is the true vine planted by the Father, and all others are branches. The only distinction is between the branches that remain on the vine and thus receive life, and those that do not. In other words, so far as we were concerned, the really important distinction, the distinction that affects eternal life, is between those who are disciples and those who are not.

Of what enduring importance is it if people call you

an apostle, or prophet, or teacher, or any other title reflecting a role, if you do not receive eternal life from Jesus? In the judgment produced by the light come into the world, the essential issue is not one of authority or role but whether one believes and becomes a disciple. Those who do believe have the fundamental dignity that matters above all else.

[Founding the church]. A related issue, "church foundation," also concerned your Translator. I never used the word "church" in my "Gospel Message," even if one of my fellow disciples did employ it in his writings [2 and 3 John]. Frankly I am more at home with the term "community" since Jesus prayed that those who believe in him might be "one" [17:11,21,22].

As for "foundation," your Translator pointed to a tradition in one of the works you call "Gospels" [Matthew 16:18] where Jesus says to Peter, "You are Peter, and on this rock I will build my church." What corresponds to that in my "Gospel Message"?

Well, so far as Simon Peter is concerned, I have no problem about his importance. I knew when I wrote my "Gospel Message" that most Christians already gave him a unique place. (Indeed, when I read your New Testament, I found even more evidence of that.) Accordingly I used Simon Peter as the most important figure to be contrasted with our "disciple whom Jesus loved." Even in my own community when we finally accepted human shepherds to care for the sheep—over my objections since for me there was only one good, model shepherd, namely Jesus—it was recalled that Jesus gave Simon Peter a special role in feeding the sheep [John 21:15-17].

Our Beloved Disciple, however, was not that type of figure; he was not assigned by Jesus to a similar pastoral feeding role. This did not stop Jesus from loving him more than he loved Simon Peter. Simon Peter with his tendency to supervise things fretted about the Beloved Disciple who did not fit into a neat system of authority; yet Jesus had a special concern for the Disciple [21:20-22].

Those three Gospels that you have in your New Testament [Matthew, Mark, Luke] give the impression that Peter was always the one who spoke for the Twelve. That may well be [John 6:68]; but at the Supper on the night before Jesus died it was to the Beloved Disciple, not to Simon Peter, that Jesus revealed that Judas was the one who would give him over [13:21-27]. Three times Simon Peter denied being a disciple of Jesus [18:17,25-27], while the Beloved Disciple stayed faithful the whole time. Indeed, if it were not for the Disciple, Simon Peter could not even have followed Jesus into the high priest's palace where he made his denials [18:15-16].

Moreover, when all the other male disciples had fled, the Beloved Disciple remained near Jesus' cross [19:26-27] and witnessed his death [19:34-35]. Later, when both the Beloved Disciple and Simon Peter went to the tomb of Jesus and found the body gone, the Disciple believed on the spot that Jesus was risen [20:8], while Peter needed an appearance of Jesus before he could come to faith. In a final note that was appended to my "Gospel Message" after I laid down my pen you can find that even then Simon Peter could not recognize Jesus standing on the shore of the Sea of Tiberias without the assistance of the Beloved Disciple [21:7].

I suppose I am being a bit petty in remembering all this. Your Translator accuses me of "one-upmanship." (Occasionally you people have developed colorful language.) Be that as it may, this is my way of telling you that while Peter may have had a primacy in being first among the Twelve and may have been the chief example of shepherding the sheep, there is another primacy—a primacy of love. Your choice among such primacies need not be either/or. Eventually we who put emphasis on love found a need for the authority of human shepherds. But if you who have a pastoral structure tend to think in terms of the primacy of authority, start thinking of the importance of being loved by Jesus. Authority may hold the flock together while Jesus is away, but when he returns he will be looking for those who are first in love [21:22] and will recognize his flock by their presence.

All this pertains to the issue of "founding the church." I reported nothing in my "Gospel Message" that would have Jesus saying to the Beloved Disciple, "Upon you I found my church." I realize that such a saying reflects a profound and even necessary outlook; but in another way it conveys the impression of Jesus as a past figure who once upon a time established the Christian community but is not around any more. In our [Johannine] way of thinking, however, Jesus is not a figure of the past; he is alive and well and active in our midst. He is the shepherd who calls us and knows each of us by name; he leads us out to pasture, feeds us and protects us [10:3-16]. He is the vine pumping life into each of us who believe [15:4-6].

Perhaps I can illustrate this by reporting that when the Translator explained to me the idea of Jesus founding the church, I thought of the moment when Jesus was dying on the cross. I do not know if the word "church" entered into Jesus' mind, but he was thinking of leaving behind a family of believing disciples [19:25-27]. Jesus spoke to his mother from whose womb he came into the world and gave her a new son: the Beloved Disciple, so that from that moment on Jesus' mother was the Beloved Disciple's mother.

Thus I would judge that to a question I found in those

other works you call Gospels, "Who is my mother and who are my brothers?" [Mark 3:33; Matthew 12:48], Jesus gave an answer from the cross. His mother and brothers are the believing community of disciples represented by the mother of the Beloved Disciple and the Disciple himself. To this community brought into existence even before Jesus died, he handed over his Spirit. [Translator's Note: John 19:30 uses "handed over," not "gave up" or "let go" as in the other Gospels.] This is not the static image of foundation but the vital image of communication of life.

Your Translator pointed out that in the work you call the Acts of the Apostles there is a major communication of the Spirit to the Twelve some fifty days after Jesus' resurrection, after which they begin to preach. I know nothing about that (although I did report Jesus' promise that after he departed, the Paraclete Spirit would be sent [16:7]). True, there are different aspects of the Spirit. Yet for us [Johannine Christians], all important is the remembrance that Jesus did not die alone or defeated. Rather, he was victorious, for he completed all that the Father had given him to do, especially by *calling into being a community of God's beloved children to whom he gave his own life-giving Spirit.*

That is why one of the most solemn testimonies ever given by our Beloved Disciple was that from the pierced body of Jesus hanging on the cross there came forth not only blood but also water [19:34-35]. Here we see the fulfillment of Jesus' great promise about the outpouring of the Spirit: "From within him shall flow rivers of living water" [7:38-39]. Later, on the day we learned that Jesus had risen from the dead, he appeared to a wider audience of his disciples and said, "Receive a Holy Spirit" [20:22].

**[Instituting sacraments].** Your Translator was also

concerned about the institution of sacraments. Again he insisted on using language ["sacraments"] that appears nowhere in my "Gospel Message," nor for that matter, so far as I could see, anywhere in your New Testament. [Translator's note: I had carefully explained to him that "sacrament" as an umbrella term for the Christian sacred actions did not appear for several centuries; our Evangelist is being a bit sarcastic.] But I am willing to speak about baptism and the eucharist, even if we had no overarching designation to cover those actions.

I am struck by your preference for structural language in talking about "institution" by Jesus Christ, similar to "foundation" of the church. As examples, my attention was called to a passage in your New Testament where the risen Jesus tells his disciples to baptize all nations [Matthew 28:19]; and another passage where, after his words over bread and wine at supper before he died, Jesus commanded, "Do this in commemoration of me" [Luke 22:19]. This appeal to other writers' reminiscences of Jesus annoyed me; but when I thought it over, I saw an important point. Examples of "institution," I suspect, are meant to assure readers that baptism and eucharist are not later inventions by his followers but stem from Jesus himself.

All well and good; but my problem with such "institutional" sayings is that they do not do enough to relate baptism and eucharist to Jesus. The passages pointed out by your Translator came at the end of Jesus' career on earth and they tell *you* what to do. *You* are to baptize, and *you* are to commemorate Jesus. From this one could get the impression that baptism and eucharist are community actions. But what about the activity of Jesus? None of your "Gospels" ever shows Jesus baptizing during his ministry, and only on the night before he dies does he say of bread, "This is my body," and of wine,

"This is my blood." I know I sound superior, but once again the three works you call Gospels have missed the point. In my "Gospel Message" I make clear that what Jesus said and did during his lifetime are signs, not only of heavenly realities but also of your "sacraments."

Let me begin with *baptism*. Jesus explained to Nicodemus that natural birth from our parents gives only natural life (in contrast to Jewish insistence on the importance of birth from a Jewish mother). To be a child of God one needs to be begotten or born from above of water and Spirit [John 3:3-6]. In that dialogue Jesus was teaching about baptism. Similarly when he promised the Samaritan woman a fountain of water leaping up to eternal life [4:14], he meant the water of baptism. Jesus sent the man born blind to wash in the water of Siloam to gain his sight; and, as I explained before, I gave readers a hint of the sign value by pointing out that "Siloam" means "the one sent," a description of Jesus [9:7]. Most often in my "Gospel Message," Jesus is the one sent; and so the man received light by washing in the water that bore Jesus' name—a sign of baptism. (You readers may have missed the sign because, so your Translator tells me, "enlightenment" is no longer a term used to refer to baptism as it was in our time [cf. Hebrews 6:4; 10:32].)

As for the *eucharist*, in my "Gospel Message" I gave it attention, not at the supper on the night before Jesus died, but during Jesus' ministry, so that readers might see that the eucharist was central to his teaching and not simply an afterthought as he was departing. Those other Gospels of yours all relate the story of Jesus' multiplication of the loaves of bread. (Actually it is one of the very few incidents of Jesus' ministry that my "Gospel Message" shares with them.) But they did not develop its sign value. In the very description of the multiplication I already tried to suggest eucharistic sign value by reporting that Jesus himself distributed the multiplied loaves over which he had given thanks [*eucharistein*] and ordered the fragments to be gathered up [6:11-12; Translator's note: At the Last Supper Jesus distributed bread and cup; and the Greek words for "fragments" and "gathering" are early Christian eucharistic language].

Yet unlike the other accounts you have in your Gospels, I went further to spell out the aftermath of the multiplication. Those Gospels never reflected on what happened to the people who received the multiplied food, but I reported that the crowd came back looking for more food. Multiplication was a convenient way to get bread. Jesus told them they should be looking for food that does not perish but lasts for eternal life [6:25-27].

In turn, they challenged Jesus by claiming that Moses had done something greater and cited Scripture: "He gave them bread from heaven to eat" [Exodus 16:4,15; Psalm 78:24]. We got this same objection, by the way, when we spoke of Jesus' miracle in synagogue arguments with our fellow Jews. Those arguments caused us to perfect our reply—a reply that had already begun with Jesus. The opponents were misunderstanding the Scripture: The "He" of "He gave them bread from heaven to eat" was not Moses but the Father of Jesus. They also misunderstood the tense of the verb: not "gave" but "gives." [Translator's note: I was impressed that underlying the Evangelist's argument in Greek was a shrewd play on Hebrew tenses.]

And, worst of all, they misunderstood the "bread from heaven": It was not manna as they thought, for their ancestors who ate that manna died. Rather the real bread from heaven that people will eat and never die is Jesus himself, sent down from above by the Father [John 6:31-35].

How is Jesus that bread? First, he embodies God's

revelation. Already Deuteronomy 8:3 proclaimed, "Not by bread alone do people live, but by every word that comes from the mouth from God." Jesus is the Word from the mouth of God become flesh, and whoever believes in him will never be hungry and will have eternal life [6:40]. Second, Jesus' eucharistic flesh and blood are the food and drink of eternal life [6:52-59]. I read in your New Testament formulas that were being recited in various churches at the eucharistic meal over bread and wine, formulas cited in accounts of Jesus' Last Supper with his disciples. One of them was "This is my body which is (given) for you" [Luke 22:19; 1 Corinthians 11:24].

The formula my community used was quite similar, although we used the word for *flesh* which was a more literal Greek translation of the Aramaic term employed by Jesus: "This is my own flesh for the life of the world" [John 6:51]. By relating these words to the multiplication of the loaves, I was bringing out the double sign-value of that miracle. The physical bread that was multiplied by Jesus to feed the crowd of people during his ministry was a sign of how he would feed believers of all times with God's own wisdom. But it was also a sign of how he would feed them with the eucharist. The life we received in baptism through water and Spirit is fed in this double way.

Your Translator tells me that on Sundays you read and preach on the Scriptures (including the account of what Jesus said and did) and receive the eucharist. That pleases me, for it sounds as if you have understood the bread of life both as revelation brought and expounded by Jesus and as his flesh and blood. Overall then I would maintain that, through what you call the "sacraments" of baptism and eucharist, Jesus is using new signs in the community to continue the life-giving and nourishing that he began through signs in his ministry.

Your Translator reminds me that I promised to answer a question. By highlighting baptismal and eucharistic foreshadowings during Jesus' ministry, my "Gospel Message" was relating those "sacraments" very closely to Jesus' words and deeds. But he wanted to know why I did not also narrate Jesus' eucharistic action at the supper on the night before he died. In fact, I realized that by this omission I was losing an important connection to the sacrificial death of Jesus. However, there was something else that I needed to stress at that Last Supper.

Very quickly followers of Jesus were divided by disputes over the eucharist. Indeed, when I read your New Testament I discovered eucharistic disputes at Corinth about which I had not known—imagine designing eucharistic meetings in such a way that one does not have to supply a meal to socially unacceptable fellow disciples of Jesus [1 Corinthians 10:14-22; 11:27-30]! Why was this tremendous self-giving of Jesus, the giving of his flesh and blood, the source of divisions? I do not know, but some of those who eat Jesus' flesh and drink his blood do not recognize that they must have the same self-giving generosity that he had.

That is why, exactly at the supper where other followers of Jesus recounted the action of Jesus over the bread and wine, I recounted the story of the washing of the feet. You may think me fanciful, but I imagined that in this action Jesus had left us a commentary on the outlook that we must share in receiving the eucharist. If we are not willing to wash another Christian's dirty feet, we have not understood self-giving. That is why Jesus made the foot washing so necessary: "If I do not wash you, you will have no heritage with me." If most followers of Jesus had chosen to imitate the washing of the feet instead of the breaking of the bread, I wonder if they would have overlooked the spirit of self-giving to the extent to which they have in the disputes over the eucharist.

In looking back, I am glad that your Translator pushed me on these questions about apostles, church foundation and institution of sacraments. I get the impression that in most of them I see things differently from what is common in your churches. Although I surmise from the way the Translator raises his eyebrows, he thinks I want you to agree with my outlook, I would be more modest, even if the Translator would never associate modesty with me.

I do not offer a model to be imitated in our [Johannine] attitudes on all these issues. Simply incorporate our attitudes into your larger picture and let them leaven the way you live and think. Your Translator tells me that from reading my "Gospel Message," he judged that I marched to a different drummer—an interesting metaphor. Yes, perhaps we [Johannine Christians] did, but I humbly submit that you should incorporate our melody into the way you march.

## For Reflection:
## Translator's Contemporary Application

Our Evangelist was certainly wound up today, talking longer than usual. Yet he was at his best, and I did not want to cut him off (especially since he was answering my questions). I'll make my own remarks proportionately shorter, but there are some points I would like to "clarify" (quotation marks out of respect for the Evangelist's feelings).

I wondered if the Evangelist was familiar with the term "apostles" since he never mentioned it in his Gospel. Actually, as I found out, he did know the term, and his silence was deliberate. He told me that when he was writing, he was aware that other groups or churches who followed Jesus talked a great deal about "apostles." In particular, that term often meant members of the Twelve; and Christians greatly prided themselves if one of the Twelve had a role in establishing their community.

The Beloved Disciple was not a member of the Twelve, and so in the estimation of other churches the Johannine community was not "founded by an apostle." The Evangelist had nothing against the Twelve, he explained. Indeed he mentioned by name some of them (Simon Peter, Philip, Andrew, Thomas) and went out of his way to point out that they stayed faithful to Jesus when others walked away (6:67-69).

Nevertheless, in terms of a primacy of love the Beloved Disciple was more important than any member of the Twelve, even Simon Peter; and that meant that "disciple" was the most important dignity in the Johannine community. The Evangelist would ask whether it could not be the most important dignity in our lives.

After I tried to explain to the Evangelist the church situations in our time, he shrewdly observed that we were still fighting about who has authority or power. Why not examine to what extent we are truly disciples? Are we really receiving life from the vine that is Jesus?

Those questions, he thought, might put the other questions in perspective. We acknowledge that it is important for community functioning and even sanctification that there are apostles and prophets and teachers and our modern equivalents; but in the eyes of God and Jesus what is essential is that there are disciples. That is a matter of eternal life which is more important than good functioning.

## Closing Prayer

Almighty God, we debate a lot about the way the church should function, and we struggle over almost every detail about the sacraments. As we reflect on John's Gospel, guide us to see what matters above all else: receiving life from you. Direct us to appreciate the primary privilege of being disciples, no matter what other positions we have or do not have. Guide the church to be a community that exemplifies the love that binds us to Jesus and to God. Help all to recognize Jesus' presence in the sacraments, despite disagreements about the way they are celebrated.

# Day Five

## Grace Flowing From Adversity

### Opening Prayer (Scripture for Reflection)

"They are going to put you out of the synagogue. In fact, the hour is coming when the one who puts you to death will think that he is serving God." (John 16:2)

"An hour is coming when you will worship the Father neither on this mountain nor in Jerusalem....Real worshipers will worship the Father in Spirit and truth." (4:21-23)

## Retreat Session Five

I am told that many have found references to "the Jews" in my "Gospel Message" offensive. When your Translator recounted for me the hatred for Jews that developed in subsequent centuries, I saw how passages I had written could be read in the light of that later experience and how meanings could emerge that I never dreamed of—a humbling discovery.

I myself was born a Jew and understand what it is to be hated simply for being a Jew. There were Gentiles in our time who disliked us because we were Jews living by a code of behavior different from theirs. Moreover, there was hostility exhibited by some of the Samaritan members of our [Johannine] community, on whose lips the derogatory use of "the Jews" first appeared with any frequency—a usage that had become common by the time I wrote.

**[Origin of the hostility].** Let me explain why other members of our community, mostly Jews by birth themselves (myself included), became hostile toward "the Jews." Gradually synagogue authorities became alarmed over our faith in Jesus as God's only Son whom we called "My Lord and my God" [20:28]. They excluded us from synagogue meetings [9:34-35; 12:42; 16:2] on the grounds that for all practical purposes we were no longer Jews. The essential tenet of Jewish faith is that the Lord God is one [Deuteronomy 6:4], and they thought that we believed in two Gods [5:18; 10:33].

This exclusion had far-reaching effects. The Romans tolerated Jews and did not force them to join in the civic pagan celebrations; therefore, as long as we believers in Jesus were considered Jews, the local Roman authorities did not bother us much. But when we were ejected from the synagogue(s) on the grounds that we were no longer faithful Jews, we were liable to Roman inquiry. Local civil authorities could ask by what right we absented ourselves from civic worship. Were we atheists? That suspicion led to the execution of some our fellow disciples. I found this foreshadowed in Jesus' words that connected our being put out of the synagogue and being put to death [16:2].

Upon rereading my "Gospel Message," I acknowledge that bitterness over such events governed some of my usage of "Jews." Yet other times I was simply recognizing a most unhappy fact. By the time I wrote, most of my fellow Jews who had heard of Jesus did not accept his proclamation, so that increasingly for us who believed in Jesus the "Jews" of our experience were "those people over there," an alien group, even as was the larger world that refused to believe in Jesus. Quite frankly I never gave thought to Jews (or others) who had never heard of Jesus or Jews of future generations, and I sincerely regret that my words were applied to them.

Admittedly we were not always diplomatic in our dealings with the synagogue authorities [9:27]; and if we had been more patient in our pedagogy, they might have seen that Jews who believed in Jesus continued to hold that the Lord our God is one [17:3].

I suppose, too, that I might have nuanced my hostile remarks about those in the synagogue(s) who believed in Jesus but would not confess him publicly lest they be ejected. For me it was a case of their preferring human praise to God's glory [12:42-43]; but some of them claimed that they were only being prudent, awaiting a less contentious moment to profess their faith.

**[Replacement of Jewish feasts].** Let all that be as it may, I would share with you how *through Jesus God turned tragedy into grace.* When we were no longer welcome to meet with other Jews in the synagogues, we felt deprived of elements of spiritual renewal associated with those occasions. I am thinking of the weekly Sabbath, but especially of the great feasts like Passover, Tabernacles and Dedication. They became "feasts of the Jews" [5:1; 6:4; 7:2] with the connotation that they were no longer festivals for us. But then we began to understand how in his own way Jesus had replaced many of the values of which we had been deprived. Let me illustrate that in each instance, for such replacements can help you to understand further implications of the presence of God's Word among us.

The weekly *Sabbath* was for us as Jews a day of sacred rest when we did not labor, since the creation story in the first book of our Scriptures tells us that God rested from creative work on the seventh day [Genesis 2:2]. Yet our more perceptive Jewish teachers recognized that God did not totally rest on subsequent Sabbaths. By way of simple example, people are born and die on the Sabbath; and in that God must be working, for only God can give life and take it away. When we [Johannine Christians] began to reflect on Jesus, we saw how radically he reoriented the perception of God working on the Sabbath; for God had turned over to the Son all power over life. That is why Jesus could heal on the Sabbath without violating the Law. Thus our freedom of behavior on the Sabbath, no longer being bound by the Law of Moses, became a testimony that Jesus has moved us from death to eternal life [5:16-24].

*Passover* was the great annual feast when we celebrated the deliverance of our ancestors from Egypt. Each generation recounted again those magnificent signs worked by God on our behalf, enabling us to cross the sea dry-shod and feeding us with the manna, our bread from heaven. Only when we felt deprived of such celebration because of being expelled from the synagogues did we come to see with the eyes of deeper faith the full import of signs that Jesus worked at Passover time by walking on the Sea of Galilee dry-shod and multiplying loaves for the hungry crowd [6:1-15].

Jesus explained that he himself was the manna, the "bread of life" who had come down from heaven to feed those who believed in him [6:35-40]. He was able to be this heavenly nourishment because as God's Word he embodied divine revelation, so that those who listened to him were being taught by God [6:45]. Beyond that, he was giving believers his eucharistic flesh and blood to eat and drink as food for eternal life [6:51,53-58]. Thus we came to realize that what had nourished our faith at the Jewish Passover in terms of God's great gifts to our people had been preserved and even enriched through faith in Jesus.

*Tabernacles* [Tents, Booths] was the feast when we Jews recalled how God watched over our ancestors during the long years of desert-wanderings when they had to live in tents before they reached the Promised Land. Because of the time of the annual observance [late September/early October] we had the custom of praying at that feast for the beginning of the rainy season. Indeed, in Jerusalem there was a procession from the spring of Gihon in the valley below the city up to the Temple area, bringing water to be poured on the altar, symbolically enacting rain. A beautiful feast indeed!

The prophet had promised [Zechariah 14:7] that in the last days on the feast of Tabernacles, "There shall be continuous day...for there shall be light even in the evening." And so on the first day of the celebration of the feast in Jerusalem golden candlesticks were lit in the Temple Court of the Women through which the water procession passed, giving bright light that was reflected through the city.

Can you wonder that we Jews who believed in Jesus felt particularly deprived of rich symbolism when we could no longer join the synagogue celebration of Tabernacles? But that very deprivation made us recall symbolism that Jesus had used of himself. I pictured him in Jerusalem standing forth on the last and greatest day of the Tabernacles feast and proclaiming aloud that from within him would come rivers of living water, thus referring to the Spirit that we who believed in him were to receive [7:37-39]. And it was in this same context that he said, "I am the light of the world; no follower of mine shall ever walk in darkness but will possess the light of life" [8:12], a truth he illustrated by giving sight to a man born blind [9:1-7].

Another day dear to us as Jews was *Dedication* [Hanukkah], a more recent feast in our calendar recalling how the Maccabee revolutionaries had thrown off the pagan Syrian yoke [164 B.C.], liberated Jerusalem, and consecrated or dedicated the great Temple altar of holocausts that had been profaned by idolatry. Again, only after we had lost the opportunity to celebrate this feast with our fellow Jews in the synagogue did we remember that Jesus had explained that the Father had consecrated and sent him into the world [10:36], so that just as he replaced themes of Passover and Tabernacles, he was now our dedicated altar.

That brings me to a related theme. Virtually at the same time that we were evicted from synagogues and deprived of our traditional participation in the ceremonies of the Sabbath and the feasts, another disaster affected the relation of Jesus' followers to other Jews. The Romans destroyed the Jerusalem Temple. In his lifetime Jesus had not been hostile to what was represented by the Temple. True, he corrected abuses in the Temple precincts, driving out the sellers of animals and the changers of money; but that was because he did not want his Father's house turned into a marketplace. That kind of zeal ultimately led to his being condemned to death by the Jerusalem authorities, priests and Pharisees [2:13-17; 11:48,53].

Yet the destruction of his body led to his glorification, and we came to understand what he had meant when he said, "Destroy this Temple sanctuary and in three days I will raise it up" [2:19]. The Temple authorities thought he was talking about the destruction of the Jerusalem Temple sanctuary, but ironically their destroying the Temple of his body supplied us with a replacement, for his glorified body is the Temple of God. "The Jews," as we call those of our ancestry who do not believe in Jesus, hope and pray for the rebuilding of the Jerusalem Temple and its sanctuary. We have our restored Temple, the true shrine of divine glory.

Indeed, such a sense of a better replacement could be extended back to the ancient tent that housed God's presence or Tabernacle that our ancestors carried with them in their desert wanderings. It had long since disappeared, but now any yearning for it could cease. When the Word became flesh, he dwelt or tented among us [play on Greek wording of 1:14]. The glorious presence of God is in and through Jesus who himself is the new Tabernacle—no longer confined to Jerusalem as was the Temple, but open to all who worship God in Spirit and truth [4:21-23]. Never again would any be forced by geography to feel themselves distant from God's presence among us.

Now you see what I mean when I speak of grace flowing from adversity. We lost much in our struggle with the synagogue authorities and in the destruction of Jewish institutions, but God gave us more through our faith in Jesus. As we sang in our hymn (which the Translator tells me you call a Prologue): "Love in place of love. For while the Law was a gift through Moses, this enduring love came through Jesus Christ" [1:16-17].

## For Reflection:
## Translator's Contemporary Application

The Evangelist has shown you how through Jesus early Christians were able to reinterpret Jewish feasts and institutions so that their spiritual significance might be adapted and preserved. In his time he would not yet have known another form of replacement, namely, the substitution of Christian feasts.

The Israelites, who were first a pastoral people and later an agricultural people, had set aside certain times of the year for prayers and thanksgiving to God for flocks and crops. Then they associated with those festal times the memories of God's great intervention in their history, namely, His leading them out of Egypt and through the desert to the Promised Land.

We Christians have followed a similar pattern. No one knows what time of the year Jesus was born; but already in December just after the shortest day of the year there was a celebration of the returning sun that had not been conquered by darkness. Since Jesus is the light of the world whom darkness had not conquered (1:5; 8:12), why not use that time (December 25) to celebrate the coming of Jesus into the world?

Jesus' salvific death and resurrection were celebrated at the time of Passover, corresponding to the date when he had actually died (although we often calculate this feast differently from the current Jewish celebration of Passover).

Jesus' gift of the Spirit we celebrate at the time of the next Jewish feast that his followers observed, namely Pentecost (Weeks). Thus we have kept up the splendid Jewish tradition of recalling for each new generation the great deeds of God. Just as the Jews counted what God did in the exodus and its aftermath as God's great act of love for Israel, so the first half of our liturgical year follows the cycle of the birth, death and resurrection of Jesus and the outpouring of the Spirit, since Christians consider what God did in Christ the great salvific act of God's love for the world.

## Closing Prayer

Almighty God, your Jewish people and your Christian people honor you with feasts recalling the salvific deeds you have done on our behalf. May you remove from our hearts any bitterness toward each other. May both of us continue to find in you the source of our life and hope. In particular, may we Christians recognize how in Jesus your very presence has dwelt among us, so that he is our living temple sanctuary where we may worship in Spirit and truth.

# DAY SIX

## Love of Fellow (Johannine) Christians

### Opening Prayer (Scripture for Reflection)

"As the Father has loved me, so have I loved you. Remain on in my love. And you will abide in my love if you keep my commandments and remain in His love." (John 15:9-10)

"If we love one another, God abides in us; and His love has reached perfection in us." (1 John 4:12)

"God is love, and those who abide in love abide in God and God abides in them." (1 John 4:16)

## RETREAT SESSION SIX

If I learned from your Translator how later on people read my references to "the Jews" in ways I would never have anticipated, I found similar misunderstanding much earlier in regard to how I reported Jesus' insistence on love as *the* commandment. In fact, misunderstanding appeared already in the community that first read or heard my "Gospel Message."

In order to straighten out that community, one of my fellow disciples used my writing as the basis of a homiletic commentary (a work that, I am told, you call the First Epistle of John—a very strange classification since I am given to understand that there is nothing in it to suggest a letter). A slogan I have heard from him catches the failure to understand the need to love one another: "If anyone boasts, 'I love God,' while continuing to hate his brother, he is a liar" [1 John 4:20].

[A specific form of love]. I shall explain the origins of how such misunderstanding arose. Jesus taught us how to walk [behave] if we were to follow in the way to God that he showed us. When your Translator showed me your Gospel according to Matthew, I found there a rather good collection of Jesus' attitudes and directives in a long sermon of Jesus situated on a mount [Matthew 5-7]. I never bothered including all that in my "Gospel Message" because I took such commandments for granted. We [Johannine] followers of Jesus learned all that at the very beginning of our following Jesus. I wrote my "Gospel Message" after we had been thrown out of the synagogue(s), and so my main concern was which of Jesus' commandments would most help us in that situation. I was convinced that it was the one that Jesus himself signaled especially: "Love one another as I have loved you" [John 13:34; 15:12,17].

Let me talk to you first about the "one another." In our tradition this referred to our fellow [Johannine] community members. Your Translator pointed out to me a saying of Jesus about loving one's enemy [Matthew 5:44]. That may very well be true, but it was not our concern. We had just been stripped of much that we considered religiously meaningful in our former life as worshiping Jews. I have already told you that we gained an insight into Jesus as a replacement of the Jewish religious feasts that helped us to overcome what was almost a sense of hopelessness. But we also needed to appreciate our own identity.

Previously when we thought of ourselves as Jews among fellow Jews, we had a strong sense of support from one another. True, we had differences among ourselves, but those differences did not destroy the unity that we had as Jews by our very birth. We were God's holy and chosen people, set apart from the Gentiles.

What were we Jewish followers of Jesus now, however, that the synagogue leaders no longer looked on us as Jews?—a problem complicated because there were Samaritans and Gentiles in our community. I have given you part of the answer when I reminded you that through water and Spirit we believers in Jesus were begotten or born as children of God in a way more real or true than when we counted on Jewish parentage for our identity. Nevertheless, that unique relationship to God as Father was abstract until we could translate it into a concrete sense of family. And that is where love comes in.

[The model of God's love]. Jesus and the Father *loved* one another [15:9; 17:23,24,26]. Sometimes people speak of Jesus as God's Son without realizing that it is more than an issue of Jesus' divine identity. The human love that we know between parent and child, as intense as it may be, is but a dim reflection of the love that exists between the heavenly Father and Son. Because we experience earthly realities, we tend by way of comparison to think of heaven in terms of what we know on earth. But Jesus knew heaven firsthand and sought out things on earth that might be compared to the heavenly realities. In other words, heaven was to him more real or true than earth, and God's love was the standard by which our love was to be measured.

As close as the Father and Jesus were, the Son chose to come among us. Let me make a confession to you who have chosen to make this retreat with me. I heard the Beloved Disciple speak about the relation of Father and Son while the Son was on earth, but I never understood it fully. I heard that the Son was ever at the Father's side [1:18]. Does that mean that in a certain sense he was in heaven even when he had come down from heaven? In speaking of himself as the one who came down from heaven, he spoke of the Son of Man who is in heaven [3:13]. However, he also said, "The One who sent me is with me; He has not left me alone since I always do what pleases Him" [8:29]. In another way the Son was away from the Father so that he spoke of going to the Father's house [14:2], and yearned for the glory he had with the Father before the world began [17:5]. In any case his coming among us that we might have life was an enormous act of love on the part of both the Father and of the Son, indeed a revelation of God's love [3:16; 1 John 4:9].

Jesus said, "This is why the Father loves me because I lay down my life in order to take it up again" [John 10:17]. When your Translator gave me your "New Testament," I was intrigued by a statement in what you call the Epistle to the Hebrews. (That writer's Greek was a bit pretentious, but he had some great ideas.) "At the beginning of the scroll it is written of me, 'Behold I come to do your will, O God'" [Hebrews 10:7].

Now it was this heavenly act of love—a love that is of and from God [1 John 4:7]—that Jesus held up to us as a model for our love for one another [John 15:9,12]. If we [Johannine] Christians loved one another with the love with which he (and the Father) loved us, our sense of loneliness in being cut off from our fellow Jews would have been more than overcome. We would be bound to one another as the Father and Son are bound to each other [17:22]. We would have found a kinship more intense than the relationship we had as Jews—a kinship that Samaritan and Gentile believers could share. In fact, it would have been a kinship that believers of all time could share; for the very existence of followers of Jesus who love one another with the love by which he loved us constitutes a revelation of the Father and the Son, a revelation that gives life.

All this is why I recalled Jesus' words about loving one another as the one commandment of Jesus. But what happened once I put that in writing? Some of those who read my "Gospel Message" and (laudably) accepted it as their guide to coming to have life in Jesus' name [20:31] thought that what was contained therein was all that Jesus had ever taught, even though I reported his warning that he had more to tell them [16:12].

In particular, they thought that so long as they loved one another, they could walk [behave] any way they wished. This led to evil behavior among those who claimed to be believers. No wonder that my fellow disciple who commented on my "Gospel Message" had to insist on what we knew from the beginning [1 John 2:24]. We never fought with the synagogue over the way to walk [basic moral behavior] and so there was no reason to describe that in my "Gospel Message."

Yet a new generation forgot what I supposed. They did pay attention to the Word's becoming flesh, but they thought that was all that mattered. The way Jesus walked while in the flesh [behaved] did not matter to them. I would agree totally that we must walk just as Jesus walked [1 John 1:7; 2:6]. Those who do not keep the commandments [1 John 2:4] and commit sin [3:6,9; 5:18] cannot claim to know Christ or to be begotten of God.

Moreover, loving one another must have practical

implications. I never felt obliged to spell those out for my readers; but I can see why that would be necessary for a new generation. The love expressed in Jesus cannot be harmonized with acting unjustly [1 John 3:10], with despising or hating one's brothers and sisters [4:20] and leaving them in need [3:17]. I regret my failure to spell these implications out in my "Gospel Message," but I never dreamed how my insistence on the one commandment of love would lead to a neglect of the corollaries of love.

Nevertheless, I would still take a firm stand that loving *one another* is the most important commandment, bringing us as God's children into the love that binds Father and Son. It enabled us to survive when we were otherwise disinherited. Your Translator has told me of a great meeting of leaders of the communities of believers [Vatican Council II] that he seemed to regard as the most important religious event of his lifetime. I did not understand much about this meeting, but it seems that through it followers of Jesus who previously had concentrated on their own spiritual life became more aware of others who believed in Jesus and also of many others who worshiped different gods or even no God at all. Accordingly they expanded their concept of love to include all these people. Yet he also told me that after this church meeting there arose divisions. Previously the Christians of his group, despite minor differences, had a good sense of unity among themselves; but now they were divided in their judgments as to whether their church had gone too far. Frankly I know little about loving everybody in the world—I suppose it is acceptable or (I notice disappointment in your Translator's eyes) even more than acceptable. But I do know this with certainty: Unless you who believe that Jesus is God's Son love one another, an all-embracing love for outsiders is not impressive. Indeed, it is scarcely possible, for we are channels not creators of the love that comes from Christ, and it passes through the fellow Christians whom we love in order to reach those who are not yet believers.

Moreover, how can others be impressed and tempted to join a group where there is hatred for one another? To be true followers of Jesus there may be many things that must be done, many directives to be followed. Yet, no matter what else is done, those who do not walk according to Jesus' commandment, "Love one another as I have loved you," are not following in the way he intended. And he alone is the way to the Father [14:6].

After I have said that, some of you may still wish to press me as to why there is such a lack of love for the world in my "Gospel Message." The situation is complicated. I reported Jesus' statement about God's basic attitude: "God loved the world so much that He gave the only Son that everyone who believes in him may not perish but have eternal life; God did not send the Son into the world to condemn the world but that the world might be saved through him" [3:16-17]. The Son was willing to give his flesh for the life of the world [6:51]. Yet the tragedy was that having come into a world that was made by him, the world did not recognize him [1:10], and people preferred darkness to the light that had come into the world [3:19].

And so Jesus had to quickly recognize that a disbelieving world hated him because his very presence revealed the evil doings of the world [7:7]. The culmination of this came when Jesus was condemned to be crucified; the world had decided for its evil Prince [the devil] who had seemingly triumphed. Actually, however, the lifting up of Jesus from the earth on the cross meant that Jesus was returning in victory to his Father and was defeating the Prince of this world [12:31-32; 14:30; 16:11].

"Have courage; I have conquered the world" [16:33]. It was this world for which Jesus had no love and refused to pray [17:9].

He would still have the world believe in him [17:21-22], but he knew that the world would hate his disciples because they do not belong to the world. When the Paraclete Spirit would come, the world would not receive him [14:17], and so it would be his task to prove that the world was wrong about Jesus [16:8-11]. No wonder we [Johannine Christians] maintained that the love of God is irreconcilable with love for the world [1 John 2:15].

Some would equate our [Johannine] lack of love for the world with our attitude toward "the Jews" who, like the world, could not accept Jesus. No!—despite my occasional very strong language about "the Jews," that is not true. As I explained in a previous retreat session, we argued with Jewish synagogue authorities about God's will, but we all accepted that there was one God whom we should serve. The world in our thought had an evil Prince that it served. My fellow disciple who wrote what you call the First Epistle of John phrased the issue strongly but correctly: "The world is passing away with all its desires, but the person who does the will of God lives forever" [1 John 2:17]. "We know that it is to God we belong, while the whole world lies in the grasp of the Evil One" [1 John 5:19].

Your Translator tells me that many of you think that followers of Jesus should love the world. There are good things in the world; love those. But the day you forget Jesus' warning about a Prince of this world who works against him is the day you have forgotten that the ongoing judgment produced by the light of the world shows up evil as well as good.

## For Reflection:
## Translator's Contemporary Application

I was both surprised and moved by the intensity of the Evangelist's emphasis on "one another" in Jesus' command to love. If you look back over his conferences, you will notice how often (sometimes with sarcasm) he was responding to observations or objections I offered. In respect to love I thought he was being too narrow, but he was absolutely convinced that we should not water down the internal love within the Christian community. We often say, "Charity begins at home." He would insist, "Love begins at home."

This insistence of the Evangelist made me realize the extent to which the hostilities that have developed among Catholics (for example, conservative against liberal) were the very antithesis of what he considered the essential attitude commanded by Jesus. I was going to tell him that many of our hostilities centered on the eucharist (liturgy), the most sacred gift of Jesus' flesh and blood, the food of eternal life. But then I remembered that in his fourth conference he was aware of divisions over the eucharist in his own time so that he stressed the spirit of self-giving in the washing of the feet. Indeed, in his own Gospel (6:60-66) he showed a division among Jesus' own disciples after he had spoken about his flesh and blood. And in 1 John (2:18-19), written by one of the Evangelist's disciples in the Johannine School, we see a community so divided that some, who are regarded as Antichrists, have "gone out."

There is a legend recorded by Saint Jerome that when John was an old man, when he could no longer compose a sermon, he said over and over again, "Little children, love one another." When people kept asking him why he always repeated the same words, he answered, "If you do that, you do enough." I did not have the heart to ask our crusty Evangelist whether this was true of himself lest he debunk such a beautiful memory. But certainly the legend is true to his "Gospel Message."

There is also a very old tradition that pagans were enormously impressed by solidarity among Christians, exclaiming "See how these Christians love one another!" Today division and antagonism among churches are bad enough (and, praise God, beginning to lessen), but internal division within a church is worse. (As a Roman Catholic I think of my own church; but alas, internal division is common to most churches.) People rightly insist on the importance of the Ten Commandments. Are they as indignant when the one commandment reported by John is broken and we do not love one another? Would any outsider today say, "See how these Christians love one another"?

## Closing Prayer

Almighty God, Father in heaven, the First Epistle of John has told us that by definition you are love. If that is characteristic of your relation to the Son and the Spirit and of your relation to us, we can scarcely call ourselves your people if we do not sincerely love one another. That one commandment that your Son proposed so simply is actually very difficult for us to practice. Help us to love one another in the church, in the communities in which we live and in our families. We ask this urgently because we know our eternal life depends on it.

# Day Seven

## The Holy Spirit as Paraclete

### Opening Prayer (Scripture for Reflection)

"Jesus was referring to the Spirit that those who came to believe in him were to receive." (John 7:39)

"He breathed on them, with the words 'Receive a Holy Spirit.'" (20:22)

"The Father will give you another Paraclete to be with you forever. He is the Spirit of Truth whom the world cannot accept since it neither sees nor recognizes him; but you do recognize him since he remains with you and is within you." (14:16-17)

## Retreat Session Seven

Your Translator tried to explain to me about a Trinity for which he had a definition: three divine Persons, one divine Nature. I could not fully grasp what he was talking about even though he kept insisting that statements from my "Gospel Message" were at the root of the idea. He pointed out that in my account Jesus spoke about the Father, about himself as the Son, and about the Holy Spirit. Jesus said that the Father and he were one

[10:30], and the Translator claimed that the "Trinity" idea was expanding the idea to include the Spirit. Such expansion is flattering; but it would be safer if I talked to you about my own ideas, not about improvements on them.

In particular I want to explain our [Johannine] interpretation of the Holy Spirit. When I read your New Testament, I realized how other followers of Jesus were interpreting the Spirit: a mighty wind that moves the apostles to preach at Pentecost; the source of charisms or special powers; something that cries out in our hearts. Evidently the neuter meaning of the Greek word *pneuma* dominated their thoughts.

Yet nowhere in your New Testament did I find anything comparable to the description of the Paraclete/Spirit, the Spirit of Truth, preserved in our [Johannine] tradition. Of course, I knew that our community shared some thought and expression about the Holy Spirit with other followers of Jesus; but seemingly only we gave the Spirit the personal title *Paraklētos* [a noun the gender of which is masculine, requiring personal pronouns]. In my "Gospel Message" the Paraclete is decsribed in five passages, all in Jesus' long discourse at the Last Supper, often accompanied by the designation "Spirit of Truth" which also is peculiarly our language.

Your Translator tells me that you have had a problem rendering *Paraklētos* into your language—understandably, for it has several connotations, as I shall point out. (I was a bit amused when I heard that several hundred years after my time a famous translator [Saint Jerome] settled for transliterating the word into Latin as *Paracletus* and that many prefer "Paraclete" as the best rendition in your own language.)

**[Aspects of the Paraclete].** Our [Johannine] tradition did not get the word out of thin air. Literally in the Greek of my time *paraklētos* meant "one called alongside," particularly one called to help in a legal situation: a defense attorney. [Translator's note: A forensic or courtroom atmosphere can be seen in English translations like "Advocate, Counselor."]

Actually there is a legal tone to some of what Jesus said about the Paraclete; yet the picture is more exactly that of a prosecuting attorney. Jesus was going to die on a cross—in the eyes of the world judged guilty and convicted. Yet after his death, the Paraclete would come and reverse the sentence by convicting the world and proving Jesus' innocence [16:8-11]. He would demonstrate that Jesus did not sin; rather the world sinned by not believing in him. Jesus is the one who is just or righteous, as shown by the fact that he is not in the grave but with the Father. The judgment by his enemies that put him to death did not defeat him; ironically it defeated his great adversary, the Satanic Prince of this world.

In a famous passage [Job 19:25], Job knows that he will go to death, judged guilty by all because of the sufferings visited on him; yet he knows that his vindicator lives, namely, the angel who will stand on his grave and show to all that he was innocent. That vindicating spirit has the role of a paraclete, and Jesus now looks for the Holy Spirit as his Paraclete.

Yet there is another role for "one called alongside." Sometimes those who are suffering or lonely need to call in someone to console and comfort them. [Translator's note: This aspect of the Paraclete is caught by English translations like "Comforter" and "Consoler," as in Holy Comforter, and the *Consolator optime* of the Latin hymn to the Spirit.] In the context of the Last Supper where Jesus' disciples were sorrowful because he was departing, the promise that someone just like Jesus was coming to take his place was consoling.

Nevertheless, the Jesus of the Last Supper who prepared his disciples for the coming of the Spirit was also realistic. The world would hate us who have received the Spirit of Truth [15:18-19]; the world cannot accept us because it neither sees nor recognizes that Spirit [14:17]. We disciples would be expelled from the synagogues and even put to death [16:2]. Yet because Jesus is with us, we have peace. "In the world you will have trouble; but take courage, I have conquered the world" [16:33].

**[The Paraclete as Another Jesus].** A major emphasis in the presentation of the Paraclete in my "Gospel Message" is the likeness of the Spirit to Jesus that enables the Spirit to substitute for him. (That is why the Paraclete Spirit cannot come until Jesus departs.) Both come forth from the Father; both are given or sent by the Father; both are rejected by the world. Jesus asserts that he does nothing on his own; whatever he does or says is what he has heard or seen with the Father [5:19; 8:28,38; 12:49]. The Paraclete will speak nothing on his own; he will take what belongs to Jesus and declare it; he will speak only what he hears from Jesus [16:13-15]. When Jesus is on earth and the Father is in heaven, whoever sees Jesus has seen the Father [14:9]. When Jesus has gone to the Father, whoever listens to the Paraclete will be listening to Jesus. In short what Jesus is to the Father, the Paraclete is to Jesus. Thus in many ways the Paraclete fulfills Jesus' promise to return.

In one extraordinary comment [16:7] Jesus informed us that it was *better* that he go away, for otherwise the Paraclete would not come to us. I have pondered: In what possible sense can the presence of the Paraclete be better than the presence of Jesus? Perhaps the solution lies in a major difference between the two presences. In Jesus the Word became flesh; the Paraclete does not become flesh. In the human life of Jesus, visibly, at a definite time and a definite place, God's presence was uniquely in the world; and then corporally Jesus left this world and went to the Father.

The Paraclete's presence is not visible, not confined to any one time or place. Rather the Paraclete dwells in every one of us who loves Jesus and keeps the commandments, and so his presence is not limited by time [14:15-17]. The presence of God as the Paraclete means that there are no second-class citizens: The Paraclete is just as present in you disciples of Jesus as he was in us, the first generation.

That fact is particularly important when we consider one of the principal activities of the Paraclete. The Paraclete is "the Spirit of Truth" who supplies guidance along the way of all truth [16:13]. Jesus had many things to say that his disciples could never understand in his lifetime [16:12]; but then the Paraclete comes and takes those things and declares them to us [16:14-15]. In other words the Paraclete solves problems by supplying new insights into the revelation brought by Jesus.

When God gave the Son, divine revelation was granted in all its completeness: Jesus was the very Word of God. Yet on this earth even that Word spoke under the limitations of a particular culture and set of issues. Already we [Johannine Christians] were beginning to ask, "How do Jesus' followers of other ages get God's guidance for dealing with entirely different issues?" And then we realized that the Paraclete, who is present to every time and culture but brings no new revelation, takes the revelation of the Word made flesh and declares it anew, facing the things to come. Indeed in the enterprise of writing my "Gospel Message" I appealed constantly to the Paraclete's presence asking that I might be reminded of all that Jesus told us [John 14:26] and be guided along the way of all truth [16:13].

**[The role of the Paraclete in Christian Life].** My "Gospel Message" took final written form about seventy years after Jesus died [the end of the first century A.D.]. This was a time when other churches were developing an external teaching authority to guide those under pastoral care. For instance, I found in your New Testament a speech of Paul stressing the role of the presbyters of Ephesus in protecting the faithful from strange perversions of truth [Acts 20:28-31]. Also those epistles of Paul you call "Pastoral" envision leaders [presbyter-bishops] who hold on to the true doctrine they have been taught [Titus 1:9; 1 Timothy 6:3] as a criterion for judging what is valid in any new approaches.

Our tradition, however, would place emphasis on the indwelling Paraclete, the guide to all truth, given to every believer. One of my fellow disciples, thinking of the Spirit, phrased the situation well: "The anointing that you received abides in you; and so you have no need for anyone to teach you" [1 John 2:27]. In fact, I for one have problems with the attitude of those other Christians toward authoritative teachers: If the teachers' only strength is to hold on to the tradition, they may tend to regard all new ideas as dangerous. The Spirit is a vibrant guide and would seem better adapted to face the things to come.

Yet after my "Gospel Message" a problem developed among our own community of believers, once it became necessary to correct people who were misinterpreting what I wrote and who claimed to have the guidance of the Spirit. [Translator's note: A situation similar to this was faced in 1 John.] Since we had no custom of authoritative teachers, all we could do was give the community our standard advice, "Do not believe every Spirit; rather, put these Spirits to the test to see which belongs to God because many false prophets have gone out into the world" [1 John 4:1]. Of course, the people we were criticizing threw that back into our face, claiming that they, not we, had the Spirit that belongs to God. That is what led to ultimate acceptance of human shepherds in our community [John 21:15-17].

Another issue affecting our life about the time I wrote my "Gospel Message" was the death of the eyewitness generation who constituted the living chain between us and Jesus of Nazareth. In particular the full impact of this issue came for us with the death of the Beloved Disciple, our eyewitness *par excellence* [19:35; 21:23-24—a death that occurred seemingly just before the "Gospel Message" was put in final form]. How could we survive without our principal living link to Jesus?

The concept of the Paraclete/Spirit offered an answer to our problem. If the Beloved Disciple had borne witness to Jesus, it was not solely because of his recollections. After all, many of those who had walked with Jesus and heard him had not understood him [14:9]. Only the gift of the Spirit after Jesus had been glorified [7:39] taught Jesus' followers the full meaning of what they had seen [2:22; 12:16]; and their witness was the witness of the Paraclete speaking through them [15:26-27].

In particular, the profound reinterpretation of the ministry and words of Jesus effected under the guidance of the Beloved Disciple to which I gave voice in my written "Gospel Message" was the work of the Paraclete. Indeed, our Beloved Disciple was in a figurative sense an "incarnation" of the Paraclete. We had to assure ourselves that the Paraclete would not cease activity once these eyewitnesses had gone, for he dwells within all Christians

who love Jesus and keep his commandments [14:15-17].
The Paraclete is the link of future generations to Jesus, so
that in an essential way you Christians of the Translator's
time are as close to Jesus as we were.

A third issue was the anguish caused by the delay of
Jesus' second coming. As I was writing my "Gospel
Message," the expectation of Jesus' return began to pale.
It had been associated with God's wrathful judgment
upon Jerusalem, but now Jerusalem had been destroyed
by Roman armies and Jesus had not yet returned. In
particular, Jesus' return had been expected within the
lifetime of those who had been his companions. I saw that
expectation in your "New Testament" as well [Mark
13:30; Matthew 10:23]. Some in our community had
expected his return before the death of the Beloved
Disciple [John 21:23]; but now he was dead, and Jesus had
not come back.

Without losing faith in the second coming, we came
to realize more profoundly that many of the features
associated with it are already realities of Christian life, for
instance, judgment, divine sonship and eternal life. And
so in a very real way Jesus actually had come back during
the lifetime of his companions, for he had come in and
through the Paraclete.

We did not need to live with our eyes constantly
straining toward the heavens from which the Son of Man
is to come; for, through the Paraclete, Jesus is present
within all of us who are believers: our Advocate, our
Consoler, our Guide to all truth.

## For Reflection:
## Translator's Contemporary Application

It is fascinating how well this crusty character whom I had difficulty persuading to give a retreat ultimately warmed to the idea. In this conference he was genuinely speaking *to us*. I didn't try to explain to him how modern churches are structured, but instinctively from the experience of his own community he foresaw a real tension.

The portrait of the Paraclete Spirit as teacher and guide dwelling within all Christians is enormously forceful. Truly this Spirit is the confirming sign of Christ's living presence among us. Yet at the same time we need authoritative guidance from those whose roots in the tradition provide a safeguard against dangerous distortions and aberrations, that is, a magisterium.

Without the vitality of the Spirit, Christians and a church can become authoritarian and fossilized, so worried about new and dangerous ideas that they prefer no ideas at all. Without authoritative guidance, on the other hand, Christians and a church can become faddist and a babble of contradictory voices, ultimately destined to be torn apart.

A real test for both individual Christians and the church is to respect the tension between being led by the Spirit and being guided by authoritative teachers and teaching. On the one end of the spectrum, those who have the office of authoritative teachers and individual Christians who tend to put emphasis on accepting church authority need to discipline themselves not to dismiss new ideas and new movements simply because they have not been part of the received tradition. Those ideas and movements might very well be evidence that the Paraclete Spirit who guides along the way to truth wants to move the church differently.

On the other end of the spectrum, those who almost instinctively resent being told what is right and like to explore all questions for themselves need to be cautious that they do not identify what seems good to them with the movement of the Spirit. After all, the fact that there exists an authoritative tradition indicates that the Paraclete Spirit moved others in the past who were facing new issues to solve them in a way loyal to Jesus. They added their insights to what came down to them in previous tradition.

Holding in tension authoritative teaching and new insights from the Spirit can keep Christians and the church both faithful to Christ and responsive to the needs of the times.

## Closing Prayer

Almighty God and Father, we humbly acknowledge the love that you manifested in giving the world your Son. We rejoice that having completed all that you gave him to do, your Son returned to the glory that he had with you before the world began. We thank you that in your culminating act of love you have sent us his Spirit as a continuance of his presence in order to comfort us, to bear witness to the truth of all that he said and did, and to interpret his revelation. May this Spirit of Truth guide us to the many mansions in your heavenly home that your Son has prepared for us, there to share your love and life.

# Deepening Your Acquaintance

As I, your Translator, look back on the retreat, I realize that the Evangelist shrewdly picked out the main themes of the Gospel. I hope my attempts at Contemporary Applications have been helpful. But I hope even more that all this has been only an introduction. I wrote my first article on *The Gospel According to John* in 1955; many more articles and books followed, so that for over forty years it has had a major role in my academic life. And yet whether privately or in the liturgy, whenever I read it again, I continue to discover insights I missed before.

That Gospel has fair claim to being the most splendid treasury of Christian spirituality ever written. If you who have read this retreat have found nourishment for your soul, you will find even richer food if you will read through the Gospel and the Johannine Epistles again and again.

With that goal I am going to recommend below books on various levels that will aid you in that reading. A fair number of them are my own. (I can see the skepticism of our Evangelist at my self-promotion—I had no way of letting him pick out some books because I would have had to translate them into Greek for him. Besides, whether or not he would give me the satisfaction of admitting it, he would be no happier with anyone else.) But my books point to other writers and eventually you may wish to turn to them. No matter the guide, the treasure is the Gospel itself, the Evangelist's masterpiece.

## Books

Brown, Raymond E. *The Gospel and Epistles of John. A Concise Commentary*. Collegeville, Minn.: The Liturgical Press, 1988. Meant for beginners; 136 pp.

_____. *The Community of the Beloved Disciple*. New York: Paulist Press, 1979. Not a commentary, and not to be read before you read a commentary. This is an analysis of the background of the Gospel and Epistles and the struggles that produced them. It will bring you into the maelstrom that gave birth to Johannine Christianity.

_____. *The Churches the Apostles Left Behind*. New York: Paulist Press, 1984. Two chapters of eight summarize the preceding book; the rest place John in the context of other New Testament works, their problems and their solutions. If an admission is helpful, I have considered this the most interesting book I ever wrote.

_____. *The Gospel According to John*. (2 vols.) Anchor Bible Commentary. New York: Doubleday, 1966-1970. This runs nearly 1,400 pages and is complex. Depending on how John grips you, this may contain more than you would ever want to know, or you may graduate to this from smaller commentaries. It has been a wonderful success over the years, encouraging me to think that many people fall into the latter category.

Marrow, Stanley B. *The Gospel of John: A Reading*. New York: Paulist Press, 1995. Attractive treatment. Intermediary in size between the first and fourth books listed above.

Schnackenburg, Rudolf. *The Gospel According to St. John.* (3 vols.) New York: Herder & Herder/Crossroad Publishing Co., 1968-1982. About the same length as my two-volume commentary and also of technical complexity. A splendid German scholar translated into English.

Senior, Donald P. *The Passion of Jesus in the Gospel of John.* Wilmington, Del.: Glazier, 1991. A good discussion of a very rich area of John that did not play a major role in this retreat.

**Videos (suggested by the editor)**

*Come and See: Living Lessons from the Gospel of John,* by Father John Shea. Available from ACTA Publications.

*Saint John of Exile.* Fictional dramatization of the Beloved Disciple's exile on Patmos. Available from Gateway Films/Vision Video.

*Seeking Jesus in His Own Land,* by Father Stephen Doyle, O.F.M. Available from St. Anthony Messenger Press and Franciscan Communications.

*The Vision of the Gospels: John,* by Father Michael Himes. Available from Paulist Press.

# Note on the Authorship
# of the Fourth Gospel

The Fourth Gospel never identifies "the disciple whom Jesus loved"; but by the end of the second century a tradition was in place that he was John, son of Zebedee, one of the Twelve Apostles, and that he wrote this Gospel. That view remained virtually unchallenged until the development of modern scholarship in the last three centuries. Faced with the increasing denial that the disciple and evangelist was John, son of Zebedee, in 1907 the Roman Pontifical Biblical Commission declared that the apostle John was the Gospel author. But in 1955 the secretary of that Commission wrote that interpreters of Scripture had "full freedom" regarding such declarations that do not touch on faith or morals. Thus there is no binding Catholic position on the authorship of John (or the other Gospels). By the last decade of the twentieth century most major commentators on the Fourth Gospel had ceased to identify the Beloved Disciple and/or the evangelist as the apostle John. There is no unanimity on who he was or whether he was well known outside the Johannine community. For a brief discussion, see the important commentary by the Australian Salesian, F.J. Moloney, *The Gospel of John* (Sacra Pagina Series; Collegeville: Liturgical Press, 1998), 6-9.